Meditations Harmony and Balanced Stretching

Dragon Fire Qigong

DRAGON FIRE QIGONG

Meditations

Harmony and Balanced Stretching

Marc Harry

First published 2025

Copyright © 2025 Marc Harry

Marc Harry
Dragon Fire Qigong; Meditations- Harmony and Balanced Stretching
ISBN: 978-1-7640074-2-9
Published by:
Three Links: Soul Warrior Publishing
Surry Hills NSW 2010 Australia
https://www.marcharrythreelinks.com/soulwarriorpublishing

Assistance in Editing:
Stephanie Williams; Ugnė Razuleviciute.
Evolving Mind Body Soul

Cover design and layout: Affinity Publisher- Photo

Diagrams: A collection from various means

Photography:
Ugnė Razuleviciute:
Evolving Mind Body Soul

All rights reserved. No part of this publication may be reproduced or transmitted in any form or by any means, electronic or mechanical, including photocopying, recording, or any information, storage or retrieval system, without the prior permission of the publisher.

Disclaimer
The intention of this book is to present information and practices that have a connection to TCM, or have been in use throughout China for many years. The information and practices of development, initialised by his awareness trainings and fulfilment of directives, utilised and supportive of his own healing platforms, those also through discovery offered is according to the author's best knowledge and is what "He himself" has used as an 'Healing Wellness and Harmony Balance". Therefore, it is to be used by the reader at his or her own discretion and liability. Furthermore; readers should obtain professional advice where appropriate, regarding their health and health practices. The author disclaims all responsibility and liability to any person, arising directly or indirectly from taking or not taking action based upon the information in this publication.

Meditations Harmony and Balanced Stretching

To all those people needing inspiration

A soul warriors determined strength to overcome

and

breathe the Soul felt breath of living worth

This Harmony within Balanced is

A soul warriors Spirit Light Immortal sensed-

becomes

Our strength to overcome and breathe

Spirit light and Soul defence into our divine

presence

felt from within Harmony and Balance

Contents

Preface: Dragon Fire Qigong VIII

Introduction IX

Exploration Qigong XV

Section 1	2
Chapter 1: Foundations of Qigong	4
Chapter 2: Correct Postures- Holding to Form	8
Chapter 3: Directing the Qi	15
Chapter 4: Meditation Techniques	20
Section 2	26
Chapter 1: Warming the Balance	27
Chapter 2: How to Find the Qi	40
Chapter 3: Context of Five Elements- Dragon Fire Qigong	49
Chapter 4: Simple in Practice	56
Chapter 5: Yin Yang	60
Section 3	70
Chapter 1: Seated Seed Conception Form 8 Tri Gram + Centre	71
Chapter 2: Bāguà to Feng Shui	89
Section 4	
Chapter 1: Longevity Forms	94
Section 5	
Chapter 2: Ba Duan Jin Seated Essence	126
Section 6	150
Chapter 1: The Three Locks for Meditation	151

Section 7   156

Chapter 1: Understanding the Mental Body   157

Section 8   166

Chapter 1: Mindfulness Meditation   167

Chapter 2: Dragon Fire Qigong Meditations   169

Section 9   176

Chapter 1: Managing Energy through the "Water Mind" of Intent   177

Chapter 2: The Forming of Energy Within: Dragon Fire Qigong   179

Conclusion: 180

Bibliography: 183

Dragon Fire Qigong, Meditations- Harmony Balanced Stretching

Dragon Fire Qigong

Preface:

Attempting Qigong for the first time could seem a little daunting, as I began searching through libraries or discovered some of the many books written. I also became aware of something new. So? Watching DVDs created by accomplished masters- experts whom have spent close to a lifetime in practicing their arts, gave me the inspiration of trying. As I already had my life time of seeing this worlds connections through "Martial Arts or the world of Tai Chi Ch'uan." It felt, as if I'd already initiated the intent to become, practiced?

In this book you will discover how, I too had to learn through others books, and then become capable of delivering my style of Dragon Fire. This book is in partnership with other elements of my system- Qigongs, of wellness and ability to recover and heal, and will be produced within a learning system. But, because this 'Book' is an easy sense of building 'Mind harmony', with a direct sense of physical development included, it is also a great offering to someones endeavour of finding peace and harmony, in an already established sense of stretching and meditations, that most people understand exist in our society.

Within this practice, I use some Chinese language only as a basic (mind and body connect system), designed to flow like a song. This approach allowed me to complete, an easy and simplistic way of combining, the essence of Chinese language in meaning, with the constructs of English. Therefore, it's important to note that these words are not presented, as part of a 'Chinese linguistic study', but merely as references to the sounds and areas touched in forms, by my intrinsic art of "Dragon Fire Qigong."

As I had realised; just how easy it could be to get lost in these new esoteric concepts such as {Yin-Yang, Heaven, Earth, Jing, Qi, Shen}, or confounded with the "Five Elements" or Phases. To you I say this: a knowledge base can become 'as one' through a learning process gathered within your time also. Approach it as so! And enable an easier way to successfully incorporate the following programs, into your lifestyle. As my approach was to discover, decipher, and become, what Qigong meant to Me! The Truth however; is that even as a beginner, having this opportunity to develop an excellent pathway, towards health, wellness, and vitality. By immersing ourselves in the presence of joyous being, through this and other forms of "Dragon Fire Qigong." We can become as I state often "as I am." Or in your case "as you are to become."

Introduction

My form; "Dragon Fire Qigong," is based on my perceptions and practices, of which I needed to develop for recovery, healing, and the mindful presence of wellness and joyous being. This journey stemmed from a tumultuous and traumatic life experience, marked by hardship, impoverishment, and trauma. It revealed to me the need for a simplistic approach to achieving wellness, one that could be established without the grandeur of wealth and others? This is the continuance of drawing from my involvement in martial arts- boxing and self-defense- in my younger years needs, of a (sense of self defence) due to the environment born into. Having then realised fighting arts were not for me? I evolved into my own form, "Chi Boxing, Qigong." Dragon Fire!

As previously mentioned, childhood dilemmas, juvenile trauma and debilitating injuries (suffered from being run over by a drunk driver, resulting in a spine injury at the age of 22). This prolonged an illness (trauma-based). Of which had followed on from my exploration into the practices of healing defences {Tai Chi Ch'uan, Hsing-I Ch'uan, Ba Gua Zhang (Pa Kua), and Aikido}, along with "Western Boxing." Through these I'd connected a practice routine and unique style, developing into my new form (Chi Boxing), I began incorporating Qigong as an energy and mindful practice for meditation and joyful wellness. Together, this amalgamation became "Chi Boxing; Qigong." While the 'Dragon Fire Qigong' forms are intrinsically connected to the Boxing forms, they can also be practiced in their entirety, separately.

My Dragon Fire Qigong forms mostly originate from my own adaptations, through prolonged practice and a research for techniques that suited my needs for healing and recovery, they then became designed into "Dragon Fire." With this re-establishing to style, of the embellishment of proven world leading Qigong forms. Forms such as (Yi Jin Jing, Ba Duan Jin, Shibashi, Guigen, Eight Tri Grams Nei gong). These I discovered through vast research, and the many books and DVD's purchased. I'd then met and trained with some 'Masters of Qigong'. One in particular a "Master Simon Blow Qigong" whom I'd already studied from his series of 'books- dvd's', led to my being trained into (Certified Level 4 Teacher trainer) in Medical Qigong styles.

To make this; my art "Dragon Fire Qigong" more adaptable to English speakers or Western mind intent. Into a more practicable experience, especially considering my lack of proficiency, in Chinese languages or my immersion into Chinese culture, I adapted my forms to embody the essence of Chinese terminology, which encapsulates the intricate and absorbing nature of Qigong. Collecting only the necessary elements required to fully embody my "Dragon Fire Qigong style."

In simpler terms, it reads on to become like a song of practice, allowing sounds and forms to merge effortlessly, leaving one with a complete image of "Dragon Fire Qigong" within themselves.

1. ***Explain the purpose of the book- teaching people how they can use Meditations- Harmony Balanced Stretching to gain a balance of harmony/wellness in their life***
   - ***Marc's story- how you got yourself back using the energy/meditation to heal your mind element.***

A brief introduction can sometimes lead one, onto being, still bewildered within the enormity of a 'personal' journey. A journey within, which may entail a lifetimes experience, yet; is expected to be revealed in a summary affect? This is always the case when some other person wishes to emulate specific elements, such as in this program "Dragon Fire Qigong" Meditations and Harmony Balanced Stretching. Add to the sum of many parts, this platform can reveal within a lifetime delivery, an aspect of- "Mind Body Wellness" is produced; as an offer?

Dragon Fire Qigong fulfils many various techniques and processes for Qi development, and/or transformational directives of health and healing.

The structure of this book example "Meditations and Harmony Balanced Stretching" reveals the promise one can make to themselves, to delve into 'Mindful intensions', of corrective 'Mind-Body' pathways to wellness. Delivered within a simple plan of sensible and outlined principles and self administered applications. Then proven to be beneficial to many constructs of physical or mental blockages. As many of these dilemmas of which come through the construct of our life's struggles, and inabilities, to recognise what is truly out there. Such as an offering of support we've deciphered suits our wellbeing.

Recognising that which is bringing disharmony upon a persons life, is merely the beginning. Choosing to follow a directive of change in betterment? Now-knowing you have chosen this pathway, with which to demonstrate a desire for change, comes through you.

Mind dilemmas affect the whole of the person, it has an effect of depleting or distressing ones life into a point of sickness. So utilisation of 'Mind' beneficial techniques, those that also include physical wellness and healthy thinking. Allow an individual greater life expectancy, towards joyful living and healthy attitudes, delivered within your lifes scope. These deliveries can come as a change of energy becomes you. Your intent to become someone newly reformed, into a direction towards health and wellness.
A person whom choosing a delivery from distress, hurt, or merely

reaching for a construct of better understanding of oneself, in the enormity of life.

The flow-on effect of finding your inner harmony, or the benefit of discovering more life energy and body toning. Can be the catalyst of true awareness, to self fulfilled joyous living.

As the construct suggests? Mind Meditations; are when we are delivered into a new sense of awareness within our body, and life energy as the connection to happiness, is delved into within thought; heart harmonies. And through our deliberations of how to attain a joyous sense of being.
 A peaceful mind allows a person to truly feel themself, as we would hope to feel within. These forms of "Meditations" combined within "Dragon Fire," were what I needed to find personally as well. So in order for me to deliver, you should also be aware of what made this need come to be.

To utilise Meditations; I first needed to heal my body, heart and mind energy, sufficiently, in order to persevere. This is the discovery of 'resilience' in ones attitude and life journey, from things such as trauma, hardship, sorrow and suffering! It does not mean that your hope for future self, is to miss out on what's lost inside this worlds energies, or a returning to true self! People whom have sensed the part of life experienced, such as laughter, smiling truly from within your sensed worth, or the connection of joy you may receive in the company of others. Can also develop their inner system balance, It only takes the understanding that others have already been on this similar journey, creating discovery; harmony-balance, mindfulness and physical connection to stress relief.

Recognise that in times of struggle, there is already a template or design, that people can recognise is true to themselves, feeling peace. In this book (Meditations Harmony Balanced Stretching) I reveal some of the unique ways that Qigong; can assist a person in delivering their own sense of wellness and harmony. Some people can start with 'Mindful Meditations' into the silence, or the breath immediately. Yet others may find the immediate sense of mind harmony, is a battle that they are not yet ready to attempt. The purpose is to realise that a journey through the self, needs to be organised and set in a route. That which constructs from within the benefit of others wisdom, can assist you in your developments and choices.

When the harmony of your body through physical applications in Qigong; allows this energy of developed 'Qi', to find pathways past blockages! Or, as your mind begins to see the differences, that gentle exercise when (Stressed or Anxious), can lead back to within your heart, a sensed joy. A personality of deliverance and functional peace is performed. So by joining the forging of body wellness and healthy attitudes, deliberations, and, on the construct of mind delivery. Offers up calmed sensible approaches, to finding your inner child's innocence return.

This calmness of energy and peaceful mind, is then stretched within the energy of 'Dragon Fire' throughout your body, activating an inner "Well" of mindful health, breathe and healing activations.

1. ***Give a brief overview of the topic- explain Dragon Fire Qigong***
   - ***What is Dragon fire- define this. The energy, which you create through the exercises and activities you use for yourself to heal***

Story of Dragon Fire

The how and the why I created my **Dragon Fire** for Spirit healing and body mind wellness. The story becomes the magic, that allows my heart to connect to the growing energy of change, I am creating within.

As I struggled in life's circumstance, to find pathways through recovery and wellness. Having discovered that by following principles of theory created in my 'Chi Boxing Qigong' and the 'Traditional Chinese Medicine' formulations, I could begin to map the energies of sensed change, occurring in my mind and body. This led to the opportunity to express into words, or songs, that is the:

Story of Dragon Fire Becomes.

In this, the way in which my forms are woven into a platform of energy, then performed in sequences, within which to establish the knowledge and build up of Qi transformations, within activities. These forms of/or activities blend into one energy spectrum of developing properly. A property of development! That also interacts within a philosophy and a theology presenting within my construct of "Dragon Fire."

Initially using these following three basis activations, of infused energy; revealed through the direct enactment of 'Animal' type sets and formulations. Tiger, Dragon, Eagle; becomes the intrinsic formation of Dragon Fire. An energy based on principles of movements and forging energies in the sense of coming from "Heaven, to Earth, return to Heaven." Adding a system of enriched harmony in balance. Vitality empowerment, life force energy, Spirit.

For those that complete the journey from revitalisation, recovery or healing- wellness. There is the added element of successfully acquiring in Dragon Fire, a quiescent-tranquility based on becoming softer, calm, within yourself. This with an understanding of peaceable can become- uniting your harmony and balance. From the (wild goose connection) I transformed into my "Black

Swan" Dragon Fire Qigong. Dragon Fire represents the life force in all living things.

Moving from the "Tiger," forging of tone and body strength, to within our connection of movements. Building energy up through the kneading movements of down and up connecting the 'Earth' energy. Done in a formulation of techniques, and derived from those, likened to the display initially (of a cat needing its paws onto my lap whilst being patted). Tiger represents the "Mother host" and earthly presence, represents body feeding, strength and tonalities of health within soul breath. It represents the forging of tonify and voiced energies, will build strength deeply within your life force.

In Traditional Chinese Medicine- Qigong: Dragon Fire and the Five element or phases principle, it represents the body feeding; our Spleen/Stomach system (earth), combines with the Lungs/Large intestine system (metal) to deliver soul breath and life elements into an individuals existing. Connections flow into Dragon- spirals, thus the drawing of this energy up and through the body, forms an intrinsic sensed feeling. An infusion of Qi Xue (enriched Blood energy) with the movements through our body energy systems, allows the ascending of energies from vital body organs, to flow into the body pathways in order to enact movement, with the deliberation of purpose.

This energy combines with the intent to deliver fusion within our blood and spirit mind, an opportunity to combine the essence (Jing) to our successful Qi transformations, along with Mind felt ability, to live better, healthier, vitalised. The Dragon forges through "YuanQi" (original Qi)-Kidney (water), Liver (wood) and Heart (fire). These are the drawing energy of Blood (Xue), within the connections of the second phase of soul breath, the draw back from the heart beat, it is the return of spirit (Xue-Qi) through the 'Liver' blood storage.

These energies become the element of **Dragon Fire**, something tangible that is felt and can be moved through the body system directing change. As I also needed to settle energy downwards, I became the "Eagle" perching. As the Eagle also represents the Mind rising above the earthly construct-forming calm- serene, meditative sensing. The ability to settle energy downwards once again, completes the earth-life conformity balanced. Creating this circuit of universal tending to our body, spirits and needs. These are the three energy identities that I have formulated into 'Dragon Fire Qigong, Chi Boxing'.

Representing the bodies of energy. Heaven Dragon Seed (Spirit), Earth Tiger Mother Host (body-soul breath), then Heaven Dragon-Eagle (mind-spirit).

Dragon Fire Qigong

This intrinsic Qi formulation I have called Dragon Fire! This energy is what I myself had to create, forged within the awareness and understanding of my body/minds energy needs. So then constructing the movement platforms of utilising restoration, recovery and vitality empowerment. The beauty of Qigong; is there are many styles, forms and opportunities, to expand ones own knowledge and abilities; into a life time platform and into wellness and mindfulness harmonies.

This leads to the development of my style becomes;
"That which I Am".

That which I am, is the forming of principles and theories. Qigongs many facets within healing or energy modalities, is performed in the collaborating essence. My forms now can become connected to other forms, in a way that is presenting a logical- esoteric formula, ensuring combinations for holistic energy platforms and awareness training principles, unify these abilities of from within us, become a complete story.

A story book of Life.

But for best energy, practice in nature or groups in nature surrounds.

Dragon Fire Qigong adepts; would also belong to the group of peoples, whom seek more about themselves, this lifes' energy realm and of a partnership that "Soul Breath - Spirit Light" can acquire.

The "Dragon Fire" based on my research and practice into emotional/spirit healing, mind/body balance. Coupled with my Recovery; through trauma, spinal injuries, mind illness and other life ailments. Now could lead towards a gifted opportunity, of which to explore through your life energy and hope for health, happiness and wellness in a mindful sense.

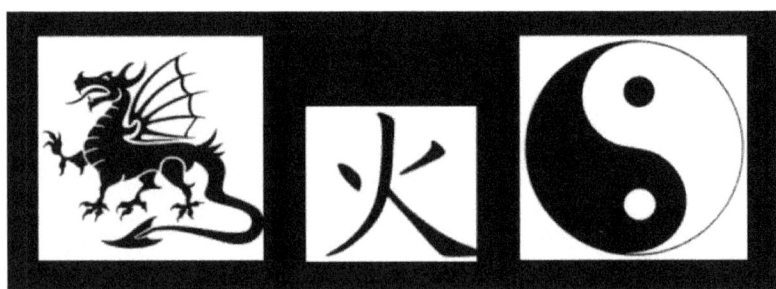

Let's explore the definition of Qigong:

Health Qigong; focuses flowing meditative practices that promote healing, restoration, and overall wellness. It aligns with the principle pathways of "Traditional Chinese Medicine," such as acupuncture, massage, and herbal medicine. In my 'Dragon Fire' this formulation of activities and techniques, was instigated as a continuation on from, the Yin/Yang energy created through Chi Boxing (the other form of Qigong-Martial), so my Dragon Fire continuation is then formulated into a more genteel harmony-embellishment through health Qigong standards.

Qigong standard practice is the utilising of "Structured Postures" building and development of Qi. Become moving flows of energy transported within the biological aspect of our body system (TCM) awareness. My 'Dragon Fire Qigong' is the completion of Yin/Yang, Five Elements and the Eight Tri Gram principle practices; that of which make up the complete holistic development training.

Spiritual Qigong; to delve deeper into the realm of the mind (meditation) inner experiences. My mind dilemmas; were the most debilitating constructs, so in order to gain an ability to succeed in reaching healing success? I needed to fulfil the ability from within self, in connection to the outside world, forms and knowledge already in-play, so that from within myself, and by this I mean; this realm which had allowed and enabled those of which bringing enmity and harm upon my Spirit soul- breath? Surrounded me with their energy expressed, also in many forms, yet I still had to observe how to heal here in spite of them and my dilemmas? This is truly finding self!

But in order to manage (mind ailments) my energy needs were to find, and initiate through these collaborative constructs, already established, from those of the past. As my mind is and was the most attacked part of my being in this world; mind connects to spirit! Practices known as Nei gong (meaning inner work) and Nei Dan (the return to spirit).

These terms and classifications serve to differentiate the tone and focus within the broader context of Qigong practice. In this way of development, using 'Buddhist' beginning meditations practice, that of which I had learnt from the Kadampa Temple near my home in Sydney. These were a template for understanding people being taught Meditations and in so doing, I placed my needed change from this religion based construct, into my self forming theory "Qigong-Nei gong Style" to enhance my pathway onwards from them.

This is the evolution of myself knowing my transformations within Dragon Fire Meditations have a different energy and purpose, they encompass the self in mind, but also seek knowing wellness. So as apposed to the rhetoric and prose of religious personifications and forge. I still fulfil, even though religious establishments have tranquil houses for themselves to perform their rituals? I don't have to lend 'My Soul' to them.

Defining Qigong

- ***Qi- (define this for the reader) the hidden energy in all things that exist.***

To become aware of something new, one needs to be awakened to its being. "Qi" the word, comes from the formulation of thought intent, understanding of natures constructs, and language from "Ancient Chinese Peoples." Through accumulation over thousands of years, drawing from areas of study such as Daoist beliefs and meditations, Da Wu dancing for health, as well as the wisdom of the Yi Jing (I-Ching, a form of divination book) and Martial Arts such as (Tai Chi Ch'uan and Ba Gua Zhang).

Qi represents the hidden energy within all things and the interconnectedness of all beings, their vitality of life and the way they can forge within being.

It is omnipresent, as it; just is! In human connection, Qi can be harnessed through simple Mind-Body-Breath exercises, allowing for the gathering and transformation of our body's energy. Qi energy is cultivated through these exercises, can be directly absorbed into our body through a unique organised phenomenon, known as the human body system.
Which includes specific sections referred to in Dragon Fire Qigong as "wellness centres" (Lower, Middle, Upper-energy fields), also known as "Dantiens- dantians" or "Elixir fields" in Qigong.

- ***Gong- define this. Represents the vitality of the living self, movement transforming yourself through the energy of the exercise,***

"Gong" means "to work." Therefore, by definition, Gong represents the exercises and skills development, one must undertake to achieve the formation of Qi energy within ourselves. But not only the effort put in, the result of become 'redefined' by these applications of self producing elemental properties for development. This representation through activity forms the commitment, it is the vitality empowerment and transformational structure of Qi developed, into intrinsic self formed. There are numerous examples, exercises and styles of Qigong, each connecting through particular points, and offering varying approaches to interaction and attainment.

Meditations Harmony and Balanced Stretching

These Gong activities differ from the Western concept of exercise, due to the intent formulated in the processing of a particular awareness training. Qigong, (Traditional Chinese Medicine) and physical fitness, connect to our spirit mind and our body breath, being formulated into harmony.

- ***When you're not well the Qi doesn't form/transform within you – this is where the meditation and meditative stretching come in to help you gain wellness.***

With this understanding of Qi and Gong, we now realise that the formulations from the ancients, in the awareness practices of healing structure and social ability to care for others healing. Not only stem from the sad realism that yours, others, or those close to your life presence experience.

So In Qigong, the self development, can be developed in such a way you and others, can perform a measure of "Harmony balanced in Wellness." That is once you have the ability to form what unblocking activity is most needed, your ability can proceed to spread your new energy; the reason for the title of (Meditations and Meditative Stretching).

To then be able, or enabled to bring balance to your mind, life energy and harmony. You must also practice some form of healthy mind-body delivery, one that accomplishes your desired outcome. As you yourself become aware of the disharmony affect in your life. Your recognition of self searching into ways that seperate from the medical; pill popping developments of our societies. You discover that Qigong has already developed the internal ability of the "Mind-brain energy" has the creation of chemical balancing, for natural healing. We also become aware of the developments in connection to health, other modalities have- such as Yoga, kinesiology, Massage, and mindfulness training, 'Reiki' and so forth.

Dragon Fire Qigong

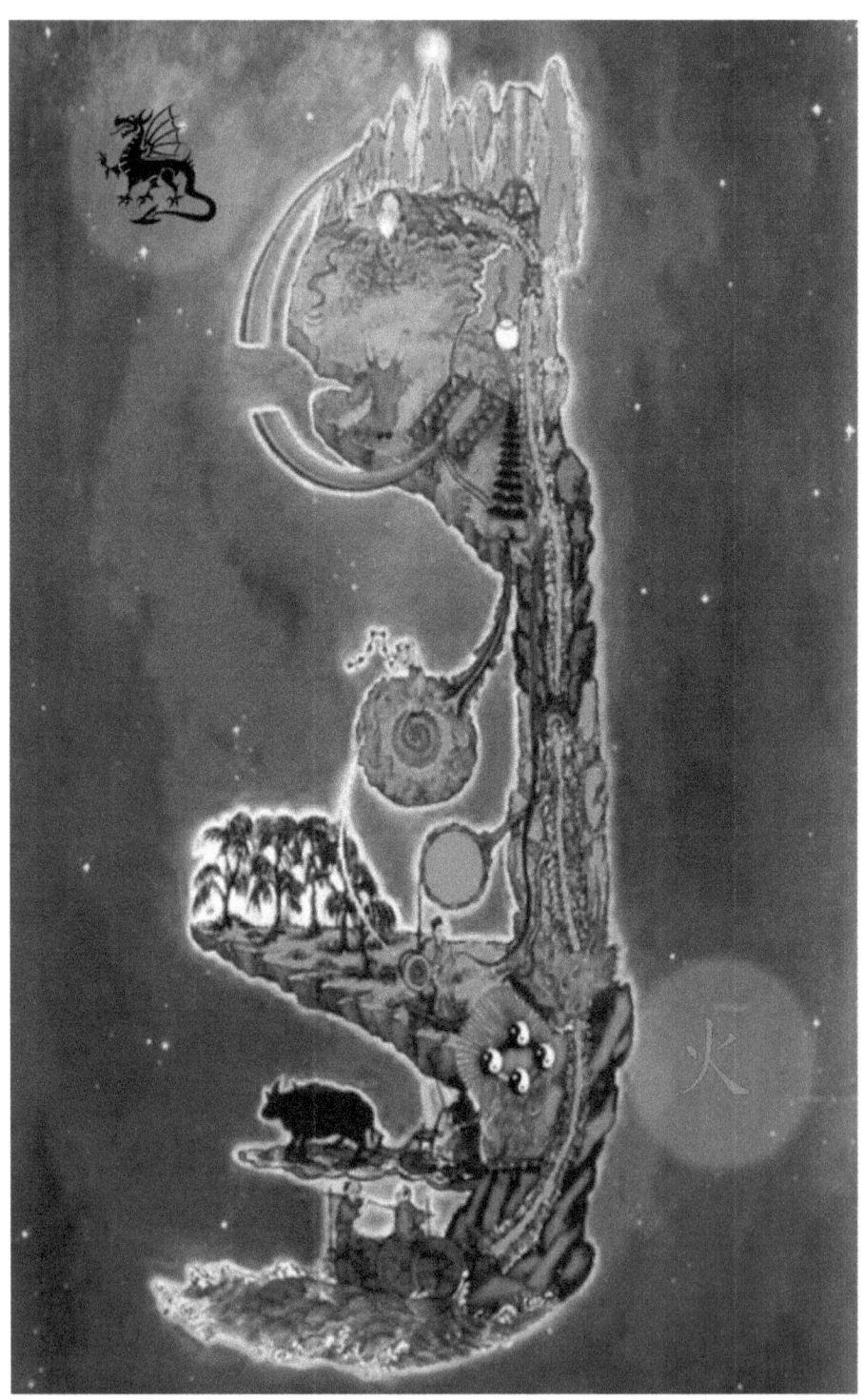

Meditations Harmony and Balanced Stretching

The **Neijing Tu**, an example of Ancient Chinese scientific and spirit research into the human life scope. Can and is translated to represent; we who look into the "Inner Landscape" of Self; or develop understandings of "Inner Circulation of the Human Body," revealed through this an ancient map or chart used in Daoist tradition, for inner vision training, into the Dao of self awareness, about our internal organ systems, that method- our living being.

Legend holds that the Neijing Tu was initially carved on a rock in a secret secluded mountain training place. It was later reproduced on a wooden tablet, and rubbings were made onto paper. Other reports state that there is one exhibition of a large metal form for printing now, hanging in a Temple on their wall. Copies of the Neijing Tu, including translated versions, are available today.
  The book Huangdi Neijing (The Yellow Emperor's Internal Canon of Chinese Medicine), dating back to 2,500 B.C.E., describes the foundational theory of Traditional Chinese Medicine still in use today and refers to the Neijing Tu. Additionally, Laozi, author of the Dao De Jing, also makes reference to this diagram and its practiced delivery.

In Daoist philosophy, the human body is seen as a microcosm reflecting the natural world. Its anatomy is likened to a harmonious landscape featuring mountains, rivers, streams, lakes, pools, forests, fires, and celestial stars.
  The right-hand border of the diagram represents the spinal column and skull, outlined by a stream symbolising the Governing Vessel "Du Mai," through which Yin and Yang energies flow.
The head is dominated by a chain of mountains representing Yang energy, correlating with the celestial realm. "Brain- Mind- Immortal Spirit."
  The lower torso prominently features the Yin image of water, depicted as flowing upward towards the head, facilitated by a girl and boy on treadmills, symbolising Yin and Yang warming the Kidneys: As the water ascends the spinal column, it transforms into fire energy, symbolising its conversion into Yang energy. From Ming Men and the Adrenal energy like fire merging in ascension through the heart/Lungs then marrow.
  Other images within the central torso illustrate the flow of Yin and Yang energies and the alchemical transformations occurring within the Dantians (wellness centres). Vital Body organs systems and their correlation to energy pathways performed.
  Following on within this construct is the deliverance of the 'Microcosmic Orbit' and sequential learning philosophy. Left is an Image of the Neijing Tu revealing the construct.

> Now onto the Dao; a harmony of realisations to instil Spirit sense and Virtue in the establishment of harmonious self.

The **Dao** translates to 'the way', as was previously stated. It is not as a religion but a way of life, harmonising within nature. Its origins are in ancient Chinese culture, dating back over five thousand years.

Laozi, a historical figure from around 500 B.C.E., was one of the first great masters to write about his understanding of the nature of the Dao in his book, the "Dao De Jing," composed of only "Five Thousand" characters, which has become one of the great classic works in spiritual enlightenment and is now the basis of most Daoist thought. Prominent readings in Qigong practitioners.

Some of the other healing arts originating from Daoist tradition include acupuncture, herbal medicine, and some therapeutic massage. Yet the essence of spiritual harmony within the self and the macrocosmic element of nature as a whole, can be poetically initiated within the words from this "Dao De Jing" book. Within the construct of Laozi's book of words, initially of no name, and as is suggested in his words:

"The Dao that can be told is not the universal Dao. The name that can be named is not the universal name."

More than four centuries after the life of Laozi, the "Dao De Jing" was seen, read, and observed as a book of two parts; therefore, people after these realisations from the person who first stated this element, noted here as *Si-Ma Qian*, began to initiate the need to decipher and perceive its inherent merits into individualised forming of the Dao within the self, for those who are constructing their way through this concept.

Laozi's book, therefore, has been dissected to start as part one "Dao," which includes verses 1-37, because this text of words began with the word Dao. Dao means the way or path; it signifies not just any path but the path to living in concordance with the natural themes and order of the universe and nature.

To live in accord or harmony with others is to embody the 'integrity' of knowing oneself in connection to all others, while embracing the fundamental elements of harmony, sincerity, and virtue.

These are the foundational principles that further one's 'Natural Harmony,' the ultimate pathway of Dragon Fire Qigong/Nei gong.

Hence, the necessity in learning is to integrate these intrinsic aspects for wellness and joyous being. This integration leads to becoming the 'Dragon Fire-Spirit/Self,' embodying integrity and self-realisation, fostering harmony within and with others.

This connection includes Chi Boxing, Qigong, Yin/Yang, the Five Elements, and the Ba Gua (eight trigrams) of Chinese Philosophy/Theory.

Meditations Harmony and Balanced Stretching

This integrity then guides towards 'Virtue,' or 'De' as translated, encompassing verses 38-81 as this section begins with 'De.' 'De,' translated as Virtue, signifies the profound transformation one undergoes by adhering to the Dao (harmony and integrity of the natural way). It is a natural progression towards harmonising with the Spirit/Self through understanding and practice, aligning with Daoist thought of harmonising within self-realisation.

These transformations of the inner self seek to achieve greater harmony, joyous wellness, and spiritual enlightenment. Thus, the proposed path I have formulated aligns with these established pathways, ingrained in human history, representing spiritual realisation to which I aspire.

Lastly, the word 'Jing,' in this sense meaning 'Classic,' was added to symbolise the timeless significance of these teachings. As I do not follow any religious energy source such as Christianity; Islam, Hinduism, Daoism or Buddhism, the "that which I am" is my understanding, my realisations and constructs within self for betterment.

Below Qigong Stance; Standing at the Ready

Dragon Fire Qigong

Our Living Spirit in a Physical Form

Other ways of refining our energy: Living Spirit in Physical form; as we are aware that there are many sacred energetic places in this world, throughout history; people of different faiths/beliefs and spiritual traditions, have traveled to these and made many kinds of pilgrimages around the world. These locations are often known to exhibit electromagnetic fields; some occurring naturally, while others accumulated an energy over time. Possibly through worship, meditation, and/or other spiritual practices.

The best places have a combination of these; and to help develop your own energy, it may be suggested that you should attempt to visit and or to (practice-meditate) at some of these amazing places or sites.

In my memoirs there are many such places that I have visited; that even though I had not developed the connection to Qigong as yet.

Some of these would include; climbing "Uluru" and walking amongst the "Kata Juta," exploring "Watarka" and other sacred sites in the Australian indigenous landscape, as well as "Kakadu" and "Nitmuluk" the Katherine Gorge, Litchfield National Park, Rinyirru Lakefield National Park, and Oh so many more!

As far as overseas; the finding of myself (Spirit Heart) once again, in a place called (Four thousand islands) "Laos" or the travel through the many spiritual sites of Thailand (Chang Rai; Chong Mai and Bangkok) as I also ventured to the Buddhist and Hindi Temples of Cambodia (Siemreab- "AngkorWat," Wudang Mountain-Buddhas footprint in the well); searching through this journey gave me great insight, to begin my hope of healing and restructuring of my life, into my then returning home to become "Dragon Fire."

Feeling connected now, my spiritual energies flowed, I'd create my own defence of spirit/self; so the creative juices began? Leading to the creative construct: Three Links Chi Boxing, which then developed into adding wellness-harmony constructs-Dragon Fire Qigong/Nei Gong. This path was my determined route to manifest 'I am' as 'Living Spirit in Physical Form. It was this deep sense of achieving, my journey from destruction and overwhelm, into the ability to once more travel overseas! This time to Hong Kong and then onto Vietnam. My back had healed well enough (or so I had thought) and my Heart/Spirit desire to survive and accomplish wellness and vitality once more, had distinguished my directions.

    Now I had living purpose! Not just; do I survive until the next destruction onto my living being begins? As I was to find out? Destruction did arrive on my return to Sydney, as I and the whole world would soon discover. Turmoil in Hong Kong and Covid 19 hit, along with my life being struck down once more with overwhelm and dilemmas. Yet! Continue I did and this time with the connection to some worldly supports, in which I could once again set forth on producing my developed forms of Dragon Fire Qigong more successfully.

Therefore, is Qigong spiritual? The understanding of spirituality is different for all of us, as we perceive from a perspective of our own connections, or sense of from: with-which-within; we have become, ourselves forged into this "Living Matter realm." Now having gathered the sense from within, that Qigong has allowed the 'that which I am' to proffer up an ability; to better connect with the environmental energies of this realm, to deeply search for or feel joyous existence, loving hope, and the fulfilment of eternal worth. 'I am' is therefore, the prevailing factor of my Spirit/Self.

Dragon Fire Qigong

Meditations Harmony and Balanced Stretching

Dragon Fire Qigong

Meditations Harmony and Balanced Stretching

**SECTION I:
DRAGON FIRE QIGONG;
MEDITATIONS HARMONY BALANCED
STRETCHING FOUNDATIONS**

FOUNDATIONS OF QIGONG

Dragon Fire Qigong

Meditations Harmony and Balanced Stretching

Chapter 1:

Continuing: three applications of Qigong:

"Martial, Health, and Spiritual."

Each of these has its own unique set of exercises to achieve their overall effect.

As mentioned; my approach (Chi Boxing; Qigong), aspects of all three branches are incorporated. For example, in the Martial element, there is a deliberate emphasis on building toned strength, rooted in gentle and easy exercises, yet becoming more decisive in its application to Martial arts style.

Health Qigong operates with forms and practices that typically involve flowing, meditative, or wellness-producing elements for healing, restoring, and promoting wellness. Deeply tied to the principles of TCM.

Spiritual Qigong can consist of a deeper, more introspective set of exercises, known as Nei-gong (Nei meaning inner). A "Spirit Mind" approach to harmony, but also a deeper understanding of the self-workings physically.

To begin practicing, it's essential to align the body correctly to utilise the flow of Qi, understand proper breathing techniques, and identify the energy centres in the body, along with the pathways from or through which they move. Creation through a third layer exists. An abstract practice, involving intention or visualisation delivery.

A best approach in my 'Dragon Fire' is to integrate from these three components of Qigong (posture, breath, intention), with our ability to start with posture. Developing a sense of correct posture formed from within is crucial. Practicing to correct stances, maintaining posture or position correctly, facilitates the mind-body connection intended. Therefore, fostering the presence of Qi energy leads to your awareness.

Combining posture (both stationary and dynamic moving forms) with proper breathing, infuses the body with oxygenation to meet the needs of Qi formulation and enhances physical development of body, breath, and mind.

Once posture, breath, and movements have been practiced and differences recognised internally, our mind connections can then begin to exhibit more intentional focus.

The flow of energy and delivery programs in Health, Healing, and

Mindfulness, lead then onto the formation of different Qi-infused energy achievements, significantly enhancing human endeavours.

Three Components of Qigong

1. ***Explain what each of the 3 are:***
   - ***Body-***
   - ***Breath-***
   - ***Mind – use calming of the mind for the movement.***

Qigongs concept is the union of three parts: body, breath, and mind. The components can easily be remembered within its construct by this format; Posture + breath + intention = Qigong.

A good working Qigong form/style simultaneously utilises all three components. Initially, we learn how to move the body according to a structured routine. In this way the forms or postures, allow the focus to be on the body movements and postures. But once the sequences are committed to memory, the focus can shift to breathe with a purpose, in unison with movement and form. Finally, our body and breath now working in harmony, can move onto the mind or intention. That which connects the whole understanding, within a balanced, harmony of delivery.

The best Qigong- being the ones providing great healing, vitality empowerment and balanced harmony -are those that incorporate all three parts, and in such a flow coordinated, we arrive to our desired practice within clarity of purpose. With this type of Qigong, revealed through layers upon layers offering discovery and platform growth, becomes more than just exercising for good health; it performs internally, strengthens your core body development, with formulation structures and lifetime pathways, revealing, measurable results. Allowing within these developments, our wellness leads us into better physical, emotional, and mental health.

Dragon Fire Qigong becomes this; a pathway to discovery and wellness, forming an enjoyable presence sensed, throughout the rest of one's life.

Correct Postural Alignment:

Correct posture refers to the alignment of our skeletal form, through ligaments, muscles, and tendons in relation to the joints. Purpose? Maximising our Qi flow, and minimising obstructions. Free-flowing Qi is important on these two levels. First, it washes through our body and helps in the cleansing of our organs and fasciae—sheets or bands of fibrous connective tissues separating or binding together our muscles and organs—and blood!

Blood (Xue) carries Qi along with oxygen and nutrients, and through the combined flow from our Meridian system, it can begin to transform the healing element from the marrow out. Marrow; includes bone, tendon, lymph glands, organs, skin, and every blood vessel in the body.

This healing energy, which has been noted from a time in discovery; well over five thousand years, from the lands and peoples forged, and now known as China, and through a system created called "Da Wu" – Dancing for Health. Healing health through simple dance movements, these peoples main purpose was to relax the joints and relieve joint pain, regulate and improve their Meridian system (main and collateral channels), and increase the flow of Qi and blood to the limbs and body.

This involved flexing and rotating the joints at the hips, knees, toes, and ankles, as well as shoulders, elbows, wrists, palms, and fingers. It also includes pushing, pulling, stretching, rotating, shaking, and rubbing limbs and joints. Stretching through the spine and warming the marrow. All done as a systemised way, of corrective posturing, to subtle movements. This developed; from what was a to be called Dao Yin; postures held and stretched to connect the mind energy, in support of body structures, creates an energy forged.

In Dragon Fire Qigong these developments have a beginning 'warm up' structured, along with other forms of warming and generating Qi, leads onto. Cooling down; balanced into all forms and styles practiced. So! When we think about connecting these elements, a constructive delivery written, reveals in this statement.

Mind, as being the deliverer expressed in functional activities, of our Essence; Qi-blood, fluids, internal organs, channels, vessels, and limbs, encompasses the activities of our consciousness and spirit (energy). Mind, Body, Breath; Essence, Energy, Spirit. "Our Spirit-Self balanced." Made possible by correct posture platforms, allowing development and proper growth.

Root Connection in Qigong Stance

Therefore; Establishing a root connection to the earth is essential in Qigong.

As we perform our routines, we aim for the energies to be grounded, as if the soles of our feet have made direct contact with the Yin energy of the Earth. We also use this grounding for a drive upwards with Qi energy, springing up through our meridian focus points. This inacts with the Tiger/Dragon forged energies, promoting the system of energy transfer and movement.

A good connection of stance is achieved when placing the feet shoulder-width apart. This brings a centre of harmony and balance when the feet aligned with the shoulder joints, are not stepped out too far or narrow.

This distance is perfect for the beginners learning about Qi flow. Also with this distance we can avoid stress injuries to hips, knees or ankles, often associated with deeper stance martial style forms. Ensuring your feet are parallel to each other, yet be aware; some variations do occur, such as pointing toes slightly outward or inward when learning new directives of stance, and meridian energy transfer. This awareness of variations is developed as you progress, and is required later for deeper studies.

But now! Make sure your weight is evenly distributed between heels and toes, to allow the gentle movement flow of energy back and forth when needed. Then, through the "Yongquan," which means "bubbling spring," located on the soft part of your feet behind the ball of your foot and toes, this energy point on the sole of our feet, senses your balanced posture in connection to a stance.

Feet parallel, facing forward, shoulders width apart, sunken slightly at the knees, hands by your sides, relaxed and at the ready. The whole body relaxed, joints relaxed, the neck relaxed. Allow energy to enter the Baihui (top of the head), as if to suspend the head "by an intention of thought energy," drawing you up through the Baihui point. Keep the tongue relaxed, gently placed behind the upper palate-teeth, and relax the mouth, tuck in your chin slightly. Following this, we allow our mind to release downwards all stress, inside of our body with the movement of the breath, 'downwards on the out breath'.

Meditations Harmony and Balanced Stretching

Chapter 2: Correct Postures: Holding to Form

Maintaining Form: Dragon Stands like a Tree Zhong

From the Qigong stance, lift your hands up and out horizontally, parallel to the middle wellness centre, Zhong (a point in the middle of the chest heart region). It is the second and middle wellness centre. With palms facing your chest and using the Laogong energy points (in the middle of the palms), focus inwards, with fingers not quite touching, elbows slightly dropped into a relaxed state—and hold! This is "Dragon Stands like a Tree Zhong." A powerful meditation pose in itself, and one of the main Qigong performed.

Forming Three Plates: Earth

Place your hands just away from the top and side of your hips (iliac crest), with fingers facing forwards, slightly spread and palms horizontal facing down.

Press your energy into the Earth through the Three Plates (Yongquan/Laogong/Huiyin). Huiyin is the meeting point of Yin energy, a point between the anus and the genitals. Keep your knees slightly bent, spine straight, pelvis pressing gently forwards and up through the Sacrum, and energy lifting you up through the Baihui. Forming Three Plates establishes a foundation of strength and firmament, toning of the midriff energy platform (Dai Mai-belt channel), grounding your energy into Xia, and allowing movements to flow from stability.

Dragon Stands like a Tree: Xia Zhong Shang

Standing like a tree is the singularly most important and widely practiced Qigong in the world! It integrates all elements of posture, relaxation, and breathing. It develops alignment, balance, stronger legs and waist, deeper respiration, body awareness, and a tranquil mind. Other names for this principled learning are: Zhan Zhuang; mostly used for calm energy balance in the dantiens circuit. But in 'Dragon Fire' I use this principled learning in other applications also; such as for developing the complete circle of energies throughout the form of self standing energy structure-Meridian pathways.

From the Qigong stance, lift your hands up and out horizontally parallel to the middle wellness centre (Zhong), palms facing the chest, fingers not quite touching, elbows dropping slightly into a relaxed state. Hold!

If you choose other hand positions for "Dragon Stands like a Tree": They are; holding hands palm up below the bellybutton, at the 1st and lower wellness centre (Xia), with fingers not quite touching as if supporting an energy ball, or hands raised up, palms facing down, fingers pointing out front, level with or just above the 3rd and upper wellness centre (Shang), in the middle of our forehead. It is good to practice Dragon Stands like a Tree on its own merit. From there, one can move to the other mindful meditations principled in this structured stylised learnings; such as "Dragon Fire Nei Gong-standing Form" or "Dragon Stands like a Cosmic Tree of Life."

Qi as Breath

For a Qigong routine to be effective, coordinating the flow of breath with body action is essential. In general terms, inhalation and exhalation are matched perfectly to the length and timing of arm and leg movements. For example, if the Qigong movement involves making a circular action, the inhalation would coincide with the raising up section, and the exhalation would coincide with the downward section. A simple beginning practice would be to breathe when moving up and exhale when moving down, inhale during expanding lung actions, and exhale during pressing stretch actions.

For relaxed and beginning routines, inhale and exhale through the nose, not the mouth. Keep the timing of the breath smooth and consistent, matching inhalation and exhalation to movements.

Inhale to add or Tonify and associate with expanding or lifting actions, and exhale to remove or purge and associate with contracting or sinking actions.

When exhalation is used for the release of heat or over oxygenation, use the open mouth release breathing, to purge or decrease blood oxygen or carbon dioxide build up. More techniques follow the progressions into Dragon Fire!

The three scales of aerobic capacity are as follows

1st: Easy natural breathing in and out of the nose.

2nd: Deeper, more energetic breath movements—breathing in from the nose and out from the mouth.

3rd: Deep, physical aerobic exercise, leading to the gulping stage—deep breathing inhalations and exhalations from the mouth, return breathe once relaxed, again through the nose.

Deep breathing techniques are designed within a complete Qigong system, but generally come much later in one's acquired ability, or in the sporting element of youthful activity, through extensive aerobic exercise. So too is the 'held breath', teaching the mind and blood Qi how to perform better and under stress of action. This in turn strengthens your abilities of aerobic and anaerobic breathing. It is also one of the ways that you can develop diaphragmatic breathing. Natural breathing is the best way to begin your studies.
    If one were to concentrate too much on the delivery of breath in movement, we would become mechanised and progress less intuitively. Natural, easy breathing, is used mostly between particular breathing techniques, designed for developing greater Qi energy within.

Dragon Fire Qigong

Sinking the Qi and Raising the Spirit

In the Wuji standing meditation, there are three points connecting the balance and posture alignments: Baihui, through to the centre core "Wuji," and Huiyin. From these three points, the presence can be extended. For example; if you are standing rather than sitting in meditation, you would connect postural alignment from Baihui down to "Wuji," down to Huiyin, and then to the Yongquan points at the centre points of your feet, producing a balanced form similar to "Three Plates Forming."

However, your hands and Laogong points may be placed into different positional stances, such as standing at the ready, Zhong, Xia, or simply hands on hips. Finding the Wuji point is the process of understanding where the Ming Men (small of the back) is, as a parallel line from the back (kidney region) to the Belly Button front. The "Wuji" point is the centre point between these two in a straight line. Just below the Belly Button is the Xia region.

The energies of the Microcosmic meditation in that case, would circle around the "Wuji point" as the energy travels down, back up, and around the spine and body, using the Channels of "Du Mai" and "Ren Mai," but also with "Chong Mai," which would intersect them both. This brings the energy from the Baihui point down the central spine through "Wuji" and onto the Huiyin point, then up into Xia. The process of forging the internal energy into our body, through correct postural alignment and balanced form, is to ensure you have completed the proper sense of Mind-Body intent. You need to draw the energy forming into being by tucking your Coccyx bone "Weilu" and Huiyin point, up and towards the front, while drawing your stomach and abdomen in towards your spine, slightly firming the inner core muscles, thus creating the alignments needed.

When utilising the standing posture, to enable "Wuji" to connect the inner balance and thus forge an internal energy formation, becomes concurrent with performing routine Qigong, you would then be creating the sense of "Sinking the Qi down and Raising the Spirit up." This becomes very evident when one also performs techniques of Chi Boxing forms and/or Dynamic Qigong. The sinking of the Qi refers to the energy descending from the "Wuji" point, down through the Huiyin point and outwards into the Earth energy; from the Yongquan points. You create the sense of an energy that has formed within and can be felt and expressed within and out from your lower body parts. Sensed as a heavier; or as a rooting force pressing into the Earth.

The "Raising of Spirit" refers to the sense of energy rising up from the "Wuji" point and continuing through the upper body to merge with your Mind Spirit intent, and outwards through Baihui or even Shang. Like a rising flame.

Meditations Harmony and Balanced Stretching

To assess oneself through awareness

Using the two lists below, one can conduct a preliminary Qi assessment. It's likely that in both lists, you could find many signs indicating both "Ample and Harmonious" or "Deficiency and Stagnation" of Qi. If you possess most of the qualities from the first list, you are likely to be among those whom only require Qigong for health maintenance, longevity, and vitality empowerment. Using a stable supply of prevention! Against illness and wellness deficiency, sets one on a better path towards vitality, harmony and wellness.

However, if you find that you have 'three to four' qualities from the second list (Deficiency or Stagnation), it's probable that you are experiencing blockages, disharmony from 'Qi stagnancy and/or deficiency'. Therefore, the better remedy for this situation is to sustain Qigong, for the immediate gaining of health and healing. Do this to place your life in order, or find a new pathway towards your health. As did I ! So, rather than relying only on endless cycles of medication drugs, herbs and/or formulas. Frequenting; hospital systems, that lent only toward medication and therapy, for those whom could afford it.

[I proceeding with caution and commonsense prevailed, discovered Qigong]

Healing from within a positive state can also lead to preventive measures. From here, Qigong health becomes significantly more valuable to an individual's life path, than just the cycle of endless healing modalities, practiced in our medical profession. This can apply whether the needs are physical or mental health-related.

1.   Signs of Ample and Harmonious Qi:

Review the following list. If you recognise these signs within yourself, you possess some of the qualities associated with 'Ample and Harmonious Qi':

- Little to no pain symptoms
- Normal healthy body temperature
- Normal pulse rate 'Blood pressure'
- Pink healthy looking tongue
- A feeling of restfulness
- Good stamina, healthy breath
- Productivity, work ability
- Creative mind activity
- Energy, vitality, strength
- Humour/joyfulness
- Happiness/peacefulness
- Imagination, curiosity, dreaming

If, for instance you exhibit 'six or seven' of these qualities, you have ample Qi and you live a sense of harmony balance. Your Qigong practice will be geared toward attaining the ability to manage Qi, sustaining your inner awareness and maintaining an holistic approach.

Ample Qi helps improve energy imbalances, and your cultivation through Qigong practice allows for a better and more harmonious feeling of energy within.

2.   Signs of Deficiency and Stagnation:

As almost everyone exhibits signs of deficiency or stagnation, even those people relatively healthy. Signs such as those listed below can serve as a gentle wake-up call, or for indications of immediate assessment needs. The list below shows some common signs of 'Deficiency or Stagnation of Qi':

- Fatigue, listless, jaundice
- Stress, tension
- Pain in joints, head, neck, back
- Digestive or bowel problems
- Anger, fear, worry, panic
- Sickness and disease
- Frequent colds and flu
- Sexual or menstrual difficulties
- Erection disfunction
- Depression, lethargy
- Anxiety, restlessness
- Irregular body temperature
- Sleeplessness, insomnia
- Slow, weak, or erratic pulse
- Forgetfulness, clouded mind

If you experience 'three or four' of these symptoms, you should begin providing yourself with preventative measures, for future wellness. Now, in this regard to your health and wellness, a light, practical application of Qigong, focused on healing and wellness, is a suggested requirement and immediate sense of delivery, which when looked into can even be tailored to address a particular deficiency or stagnation, one that has become apparent from sorting through this list.

If you have 'five or more' symptoms, then the prognosis would indicate a more immediate need for elemental energy revitalisation, such as the "Five Element Meditation" along with "Vital Body Qi Wash-Five elements" or "Guigen" revitalise or harmony balanced practices.

This, along with many other techniques aimed at opening up Qi energy channels, or warming up the body and joints to harvest Qi energies, from deep within, enhances the self-healing properties of the human body system. This creates what is necessary for the continuation of your living presence, with the optimal benefits and rewards of self-management, towards health, wellness, and leads more on-towards a joyous sense of existence.

Circadian - Clock

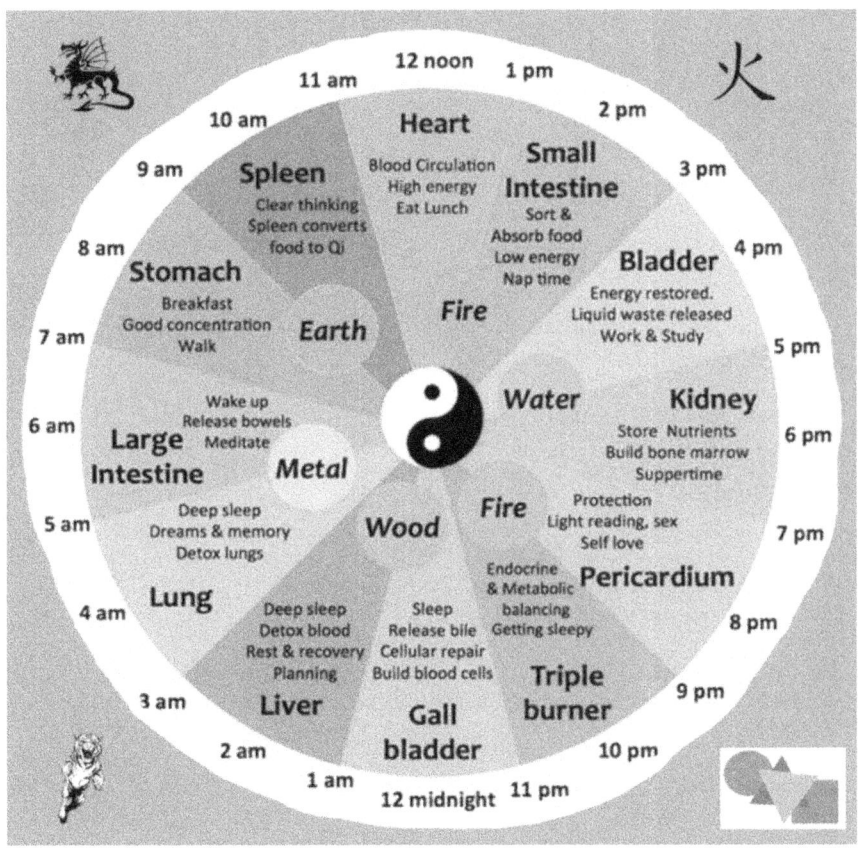

Chapter 3: Directing the Qi

1. *Your mind has to know why you're directing Qi*

Qi in its fundamental reality is natural and coexists within our embodiment of instigating form by action. By the mere reality of being in everything existing and by that; all you do, become- and function as, is filled with Qi. So too, does Qi transform into the varied essence performed (Jing) of bodily make up. Our organs, glands, cells, blood and tissue, exude Qi in their particular construct through "Jing- energy." As do the points of energy (acupoints) and the pathways of Mai and Meridian, our Qi fields-reservoirs- Xia, Zhong, Shang, also formulate with their particular Qi. Along with the forms and practices of "Dragon Fire Qigong," they which help create new energy and/or manipulate or distribute needed change.

As the direction of Qi is now known to occur through the field of thought also. Our directives are to progress in an assistance method for future healing, wellness or discovery of self. We can recognise that levels of Qi development, for the principled practice of Qigong, will differ depending on the state of your health or embodiment of informed function. So as we would discover with logic; healthy people have less obstruction to wellness and harmony, show less signs of Qi deficiency or blockage, than an individual under stress, anxiety, or illness would. Those that have an obvious injury can be deemed as knowing; what attempt or pathway they need to seek for betterment, wellness or healing.

However, if your health being under stress or injury, has led to blockages; your goal then is to heal, restore, and recover. So; through the process of transformational Qi energy, we aim for the betterment of health, body, and Spirit/Self. As within itself, when pain or disease caused by these deficiencies or disharmonies, have created the need for healing, and then with specific direction, transfusion or through intrinsic Qi transformation, becomes more beneficial to achieving your goal of healing.

This level of focus, requires the (Heart, Mind, Body) within a coordination of these needs, to develop through their specific and localised attention.

Directing the Qi requires the ability to remain attuned to a particular focus, and, through self-mastery and mindful intent, to utilise forms such as; Microcosmic Orbit Meditations (Fire, Water, Wind); Macrocosmic Orbit, through our limbs and body "Qi Jing Ba Mai) or Channel and Gate breathing (Chong Mai), in reservoirs forming energies (Xia, Zhong, Shang), allow for the accessing of this energy, and to distribute the Qi energy throughout the human body system; directly to a part, place, or presentation of need.

2. ***how to do it - The Microcosmic orbit and the energy zones of the body***

The Qigong cultivation practices presented in these books—[*Chi Boxing; Dragon Fire Qigong; Nei Gong and Meditations Harmony Forged Five Elements, Meditation Harmony and Balance*]—teach Heavenly and Microcosmic Orbit stimulations, of which allows the internal body landscape to become healthy and harmonised, within these external environments, leading? Ultimately, onto what we can then allow our energies to merge within, this 'Universe'.

Heavenly Orbit or Microcosmic Orbit:

As discussed and revealed through the "Dragon Fire Qigong/Nei Gong," the practice of Daoist Qigong reveals the intricate sensing of those who employ these techniques in a pathway of life, learning, and harmonising into the essence of being. It connects to the greater purpose of all Qigong, allowing the movements and structured transformation of intrinsic Qi-forming energies, to become platforms for our "Healing, Wellness, and Joyful Being."
    This Spirit/Self connection to life, the universe, and everything; in the context of the Way- or Dao -is symbolised in every aspect of Qigong and the metaphysical elements of Spirit/Self-searching for worth and betterment.

This leads onto the partnership, that as an individual element of being, can aspire to, in the significant elemental sense of becoming; the "Eternal Spirit" of an absolute connection, and into what I have constructed within my concept 'Dragon Fire' as to the theories of the "One Light!" An energy known as Qi encompasses everything living or inanimate, connecting all things in being, as is with another known connection, together all the minds within this earthly natures realm, an entity known as a 'one conscious mind' these forging aspects of total consciousness, of our spirit mind and will (Yi); are included within the animal kingdoms and human kind. As too through the void of space, these energies are, due to the forming of and from within absolute existence.

The harmonising element of the Heavenly and Microcosmic Orbit, allows an individual to evolve the sensing of inner being, through the natural elemental properties governed by nature. Yin and Yang and in this natural sense, of which all existence is incorporated-formation. So then, as Spirit does not belong to Nature in the sense of the need to eat, breathe, or become satiated by wanting more. Spirit, when connected to the human body, has to undergo the elements through which human form can be subjected to.
    Therefore, the elements of suffering, pain, sorrow, illness, or as in a peak physical performance; along with contemplative sensing and joyful presence, instil indifference into the human factor, allowing many forms of exchange to be performed.

Yet, with the harmony enwrapped in Microcosmic/Heavenly Orbit Qigong, this technique allows our sensing to become internally connected, to our mind/body system and our sense of greater yearning to transcend temporal moments.

This flow of energies—Yang up the back of the spine using Du Mai, to connect with Yin energy, as it then descends the front of our body. Ren Mai; connects the life force energy associated within all Yin aspects, of our vital body's major organ system, to Nourish in. To this associated presence of a collective Yin/Yang bodily function, Yang organs in association represent cleanse/release.

As Qi energy is likened to the flowing aspect of water, rising up the back of the spine (like evaporation towards the heavens-cloud, rain-sky) around the head and down the front, like a waterfall of living essence within. Stimulating and balancing its energy system enables the blood to flow smoothly, the organs to function optimally, and the body to restore natural harmony. It also helps calm the emotions (represented in the inner fire and thought) as the mind is not distracted by imbalances.

This Heavenly Orbit (generally standing also utilising arms and legs) and Microcosmic Orbit, utilising the circulation of the spine back and front energies, in resemblance? Just like in a large living Taiji symbol and likened to an ecosystem, with constantly flowing energy around the body. With these energies working on many different levels becoming; as if ? Every cell of the body becomes like a tiny moving Taiji. When our Qi or energy is weak, this orbit doesn't flow as smoothly, then we recognise our quality of life is diminished, time to restructure- with Qigong we alter.

So! Now belongs: The ultimate aim of our sensing, the essence of our existence, is to allow our internal microenvironment, to harmonise with the external macrocosmic/macro environment. Through our work and positive actions, we can accumulate self worth within and around us. This enables us to realise ourselves as this performing of lifes harmony, in living Spirit/Self formed.

Meditations Harmony and Balanced Stretching

Circulation Breath in Microcosmic Orbit

Du Mai/Ren Mai (governing and conception vessels).

As the Microcosmic orbit represents the circulation of Qi and Jing (essence) energy passing up the spine and around the head, to descend back down the front of our body and spine. We incorporate this as a pathway for energy to be filled in, like a channeling Vessel (Mai), delivering benefit for the rest of our body, Vital organs and their connection to vitality and health. This circulation and absorption of energy, keeps us in a balanced state of wellness and harmony.

If we also add the delivery of thought along with breath sequencing to these pathways circulating, we gain a delivery that is both generating our sense of Mind/Spirit with the energy of our Soul/Breath body. To incorporate these systems better, we also need to understand some of the 'Philosophy and Theology' that supports these techniques. The simplest way to perform the Microcosmic Orbit is with the beginning pathways of mind/breath sequencing.

This circulation breath sequence delivers an understanding of the points (Meridian, body and Acupoints) that produce the formulation. As we can sit or stand to perform circulation breath, it is best to decide and then get ready. Make sure you are relaxed and settled before you start.

The points of delivery are firstly "Huiyin" point (Ren Mai 1) the settling and/or starting point of our Yin energy. It is described as 'between the anus and the genitals' in a place of energy Huiyin (perineum). This guidance to feel the point, is to first squeeze the anus internally, lifting upwards gently, thus making the connection pass onto Huiyin. Once you have sensed this region, you then meditate on the Huiyin point in order to gain a deeper sensed feeling.

Then the second point of sensed feeling is the "Baihui" point, Du Mai 20. It is on top of the head, just behind the crown. This point is the Yang meridian and energy connection place called '100 meeting place'. It is the connection point also to our cosmic spirit connect. Where the energy of the cosmos can connect down and to within us (Crown), so by tucking in your chin slightly forging. Meditate on this point to sense the place of/or a cap, for our body energy.

Thirdly is "Xia" the (lower wellness centre) or Dantien. This is the point on the Ren Mai {female Qi Hai 6 Uterus, Male Ren Mai 3-4 Prostate}. But in Qigong it is regarded as the point where energy accumulates into a growing field, to then be moved through the body energy systems. It is called the first energy field, as it is also where the accumulation of energy from the umbilical, helped to form us into being. This is found below the belly button 3-5 finger widths- post heaven, internally toward spine pre-heaven. Energy comes in, sinks, forges and then is distributed throughout the body (pre-heaven). Post-heaven is through the generate our life, or sexual formulation connect, 'uterus female, prostate male- ductus Vas deferens- seminal vesicle' in our energy forming. Once you have the understanding of where these points are on the body, we begin to circulate our mindful breath along this circuit.

Starting breath-mind, from 'Huiyin' up along the rear spine-back, connecting through 'Du mai' Yang energy. Connect to Baihui as the breath fulfils. Downwards we descend the breath into the Xia region, before completing the circuit back at Huiyin. Each circulation breath is breathe in upwards, breathe out downwards. Up through the back, down through the front, do this a few times to find your energy.

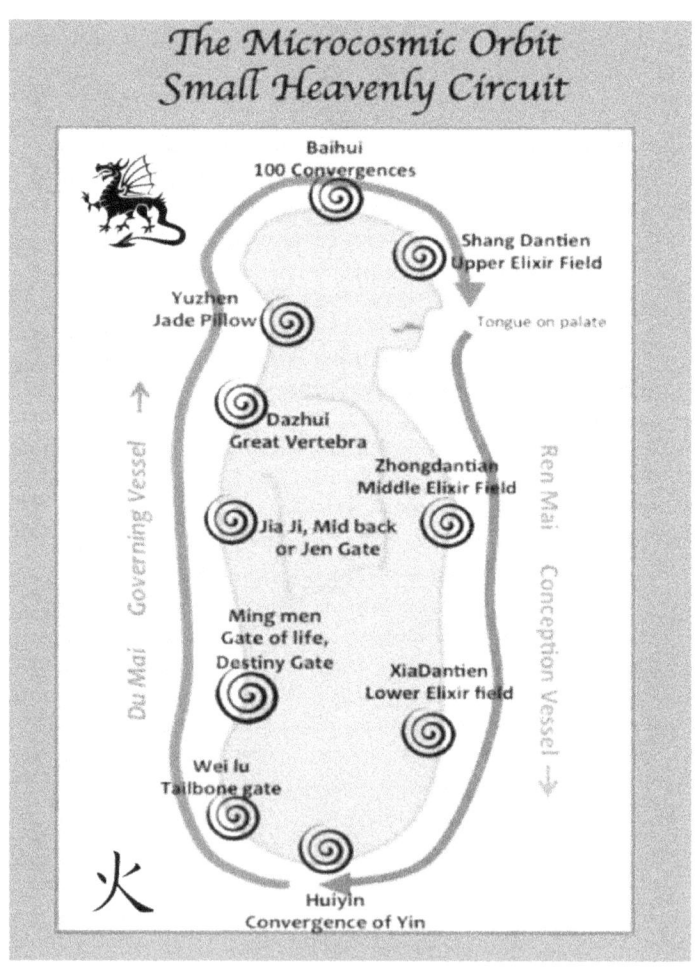

Meditations Harmony and Balanced Stretching

Chapter 4: Meditation Techniques
1. ***The 3 Channels***
   - **Chong Mai 'sea of blood'**
   - **Ren Mai 'sea of Yin'**
   - **Du Mai 'sea of Yang'**

Du Mai and Ren Mai:

The Du Mai (Governing) and Ren Mai (Conception) are the two main major energy vessels that run along the central core of our body (spine), separating the body into the front and back of our spine. The focus in this technique is to connect the sequential flow of circulation through the main and major energy points; in this circulation of mind/breath intent. Use your awareness to concentrate on these energy centres around the orbit. A basic principle in this Qigong awareness maintains the adage, 'where the mind goes the Qi follows'. As Qi flows naturally around this orbit, our job is to strengthen this flow. It's important not to try too hard in this delivery, but to relax, allow the feel of each energy point described. Make the connection through your senses, add on from the previous form 'circulation breath' to go deeper into these Vessels.

In connection to these energy circuits belong the belt vessels - **Dai Mai;** from the bellybutton around to the kidney region - Ming Men, and back in a ring or belt + upper and lower wellness centres Xia-Shang. These involve circles around key points on the body, pivotal to energy zones.

Chong Mai (Wind): (Penetrating vessel) runs straight down the middle of the spine, from 'Baihui-Crown' (in this case, meaning sky door) at the top of the head on the Du Mai, straight down to Huiyin, the Yin energy meeting point on the Ren Mai, and then onto Xia. Connects the Kidneys to Xia, ascends to the face from abdomen starting point ST-30 Qichong, and then after reaching the face, descends through the trunk and legs to the toes, connects more deeply with Ren mai.

In Dragon Fire it is the "Wind," breath-mind circulation in the energy of movement exchange meditations; it connects as 'The Sea of Blood' meaning 'Uterus and blood channels'. Deep connection to the Heart and Chong Mai as the heart governs blood, as it is in the centre of the energy vortex (Du, Chong, Ren Mai) it is strongly related to the Liver due to its path down the legs and its connection through the abdomen (rectus abdominis) Ancestral muscles- Zong jin and reproduction centre- male (prostate) and female (uterus). This vessel "Chong Mai"connects the Pre- Heaven (Kidney) and Post- Heaven Qi (Stomach), which allows 'Essence' (Jing) to travel within the body, and has other named connections as: "sea of Blood" "Sea of 12 Vessels" and its influence connection to "Sea of the Five Yin and Six Yang Organs."

Du Mai (Fire): The Du Mai distributes Qi energy in an ascending flow, from the lower point known as Weilu (coccyx) up various points along the back of the spine. Next is Ming Men (gate of life fire) in the kidney region, followed by Dazhui (great hammer) region behind the heart and between the shoulder blades, acts as a crux through arms and shoulders- Du Mai 14 , an area of great strength. Continuing up, Yuzhen (jade cushion) is reached, where many energies pass through (Cranial Pump), serving as the soft connect of the skull and neck. Further up is Baihui (crown of the head), then Shang (upper wellness centre), a point in the middle of the forehead, and finally down to a point in the upper lip, ending the "Du Mai."

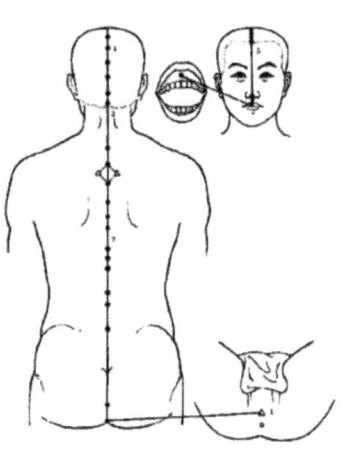

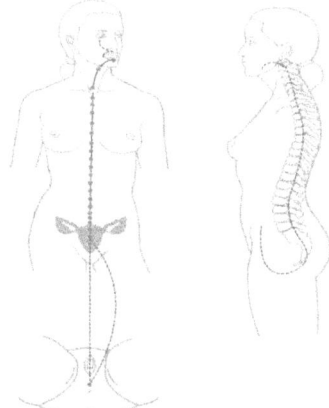

Ren Mai (Water): The Ren Mai distributes Qi energy in an ascending flow up the front of the spine from the area known as Huiyin (perineum), which is the Yin energy meeting point on the "Ren Mai" (conception vessel). Its energy delivered from Huiyin (the point between the anus and genitals) up through the lower wellness centre Xia, the middle wellness centre Zhong, to a point below the lower lip. As it connects to the '**Fire circuit**'. It also descends from the mouth downwards into Xia and onwards to "Huiyin" representing the phase of feeding the body self. These two important vessels have several functions, including feeding Qi energy into all the other meridians, directly influencing the Yin/Yang organs of the "five elements table," and directing the flow of Qi energy through the meridians and through the 'Microcosmic orbit and Macrocosmic orbit' of mindful intent.

2. *Heart mind- the commander of Qi*

Heart Mind (Xin)

Heart/Mind is the Commander of Qi: In Traditional Chinese Medicine (TCM) and philosophy, 'the Mind is the leader of Qi.' In general terms, this means the Heart, in its integrated relationship with the Mind, leads the Qi. Therefore, in Chinese thought, there is only Xin ('Heart/Mind'). This same sentiment is also stated as 'Qi follows intention,' whether it is by placing hands on points, centres of life energy, or using mind intention. Directing Qi requires a greater degree of focus and intention than needed for the beginning phases of learning Qigong.

The level of mind focus and clarity necessary to 'Direct Qi' is greater than simple relaxation. It is necessary to train the Heart/Mind (Xin) to sustain a single focus for an extended period of time, as in meditations, complete forms or principle platform fulfilment structures.

This is why 'Directing Qi' serves as the bridge between initial, more simplistic Qigong practiced and more advanced 'Practitioners', experienced cultivation.

With Intention and Will ('Yi!'), no matter what methods are used to direct Qi, sustained calm focus of the Heart/Mind will maximise the effect. This sense of listening to the Heart (feelings) in meditation or visualisation brings focused intention to the Heart/Mind (Xin). When Directing Qi, sensitivity (Xin) and willpower (Yi) enhance the effect because a focused 'Mind leads Qi' more proficiently.

Breathe: Use the breath to guide Qi to specific destinations, particularly on exhalation. The simplest practice is to gather and concentrate inner resources on inhalation (filling Wellness Centres) and direct this energy on exhalation.

Remember that a clear, calm Heart/Mind connection allows better guidance of Qi. Some of the best ways to direct Qi are with massage, hand placement, or tracing the energy channels. With massage or near touch, use your Heart/Mind intent to direct Qi to your hands via 'Laogong and Hegu' energy points. Then, by tracing, touching, rubbing, tapping, or just holding the presence of energy onto or within an area or centre (infuse Self with Qi forming).

Dragon Fire Qigong

Meditations Harmony and Balanced Stretching

Dragon Fire Qigong

SECTION II:

DRAGON FIRE QIGONG

MEDITATIONS HARMONY BALANCED

STRETCHING

WARMING THE BALANCE AND QI

Chapter 1:

Warming The Balance: of (Body; Breath and Mind, for practice)

The first stage of preparation is to warm the body, joints, and limbs for receiving Qi flow. When the body has been sufficiently warmed by stretching muscles and tendons, loosening joints and vertebrae, and releasing all physical tension, warming the circulation and activating the endocrine system, as well as opening the energy channels (Mai, Meridian and pathways) in readiness for the main practice forms, one can then move on to the second of three stages, the moving of energy-meditation or Dynamic Qigong.

This second stage refers to the cultivation of body, mind, breath, and Qi energy, awakened from within. Using forms of standing and moving practice, 'Dynamic Qigong' can bring to oneself the cultivation of these intrinsic energies, the forging of body and essence. In seated forms definitive "Jin" warming or as they say 'warming the juice of the spine' helps to deliver the correct formulations of energy transfer, required to complete proper transference harmony. After completing some of the many moving meditations and energy-raising forms, we then need to reach a stage in partnership from each of these actions, thus the need for a third stage of any practice.

The third stage of any practice routine should always include collecting and storing these energies, in the calming and cooling-down period; which can lead to Stretching forms; Stillness meditation forms or Tranquil Nei Gong, of which the growing of Essence and Energy into Energy and Spirit are performed.

First page of images is for the Opening into: Dragon connects mind to body Kua form. Designed to ready the body for connection to your movement pathways.

Meditations Harmony and Balanced Stretching

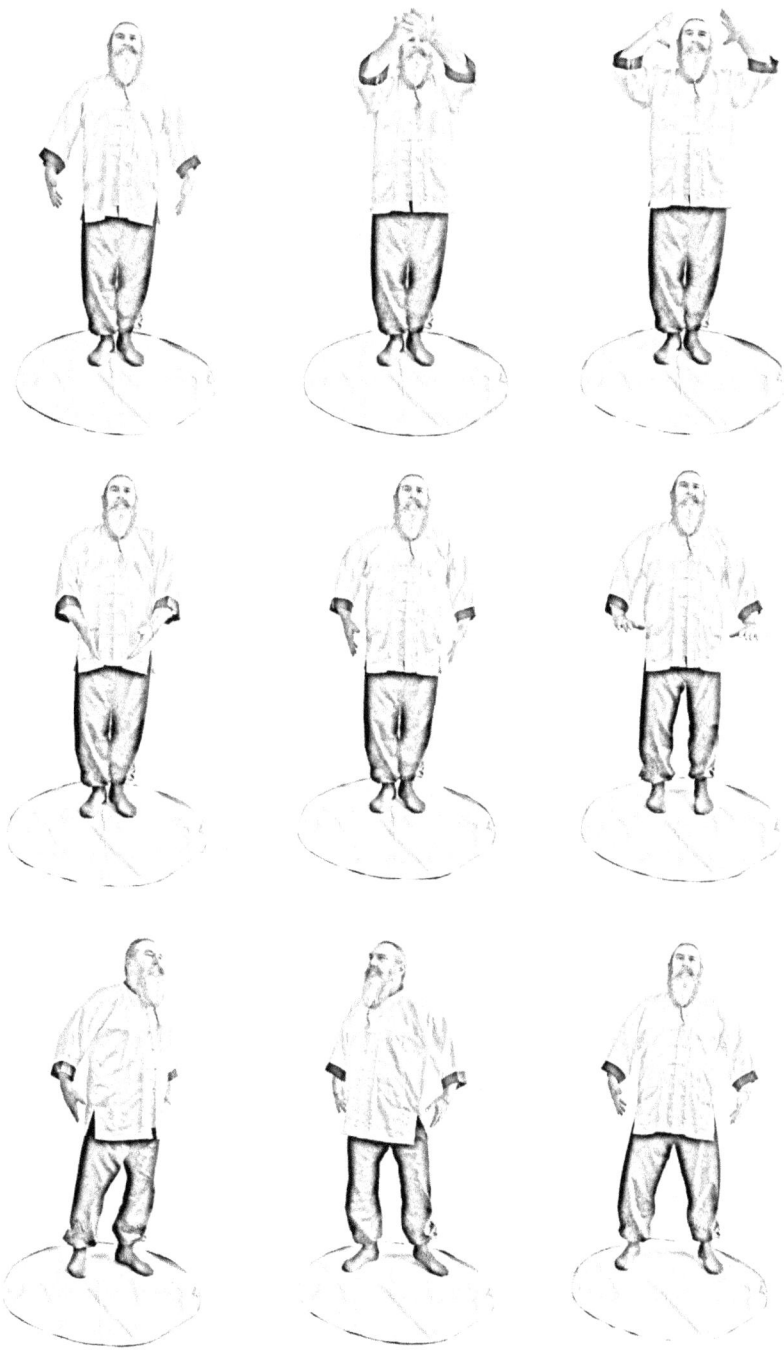

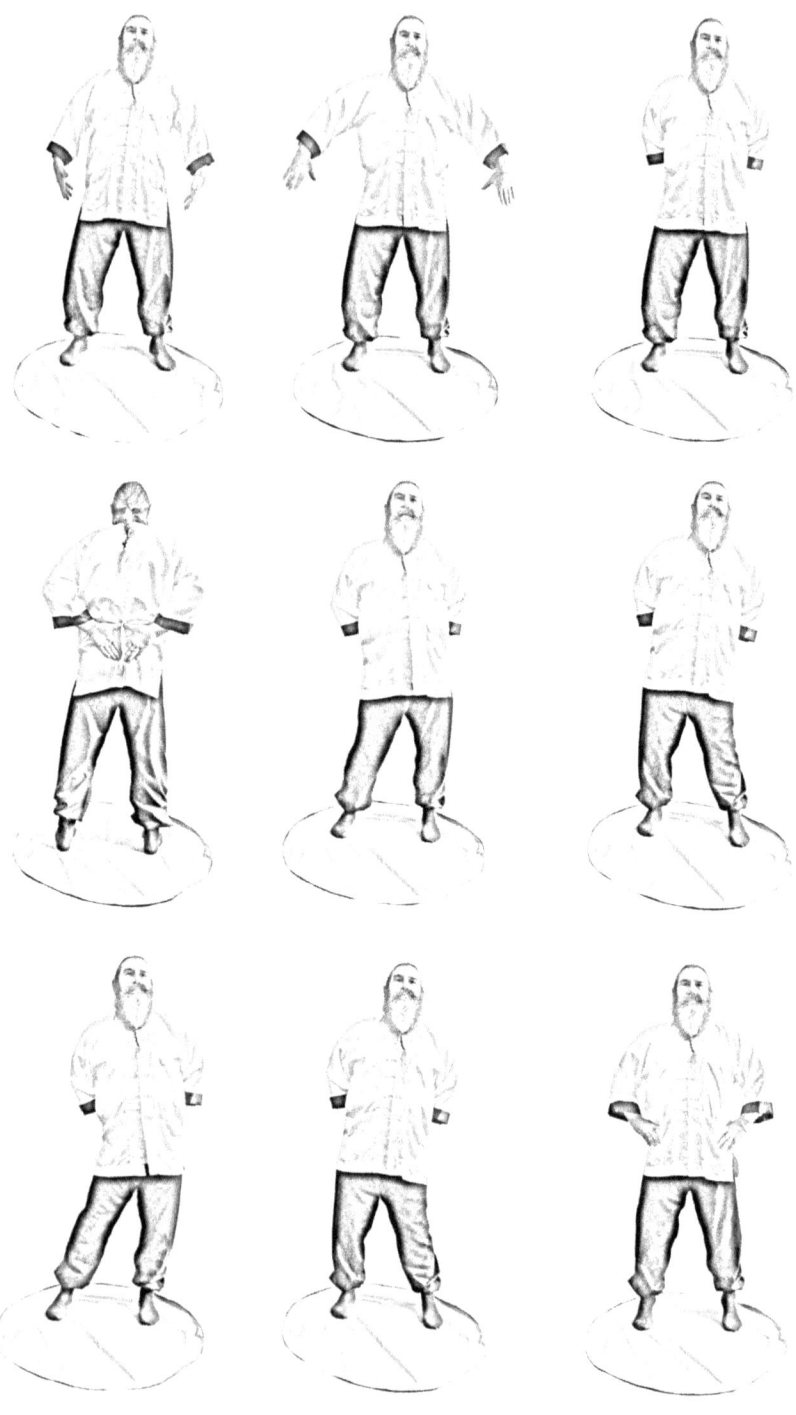

Meditations Harmony and Balanced Stretching

Dragon Fire Qigong

Meditations Harmony and Balanced Stretching

Dragon Fire Qigong

Meditations Harmony and Balanced Stretching

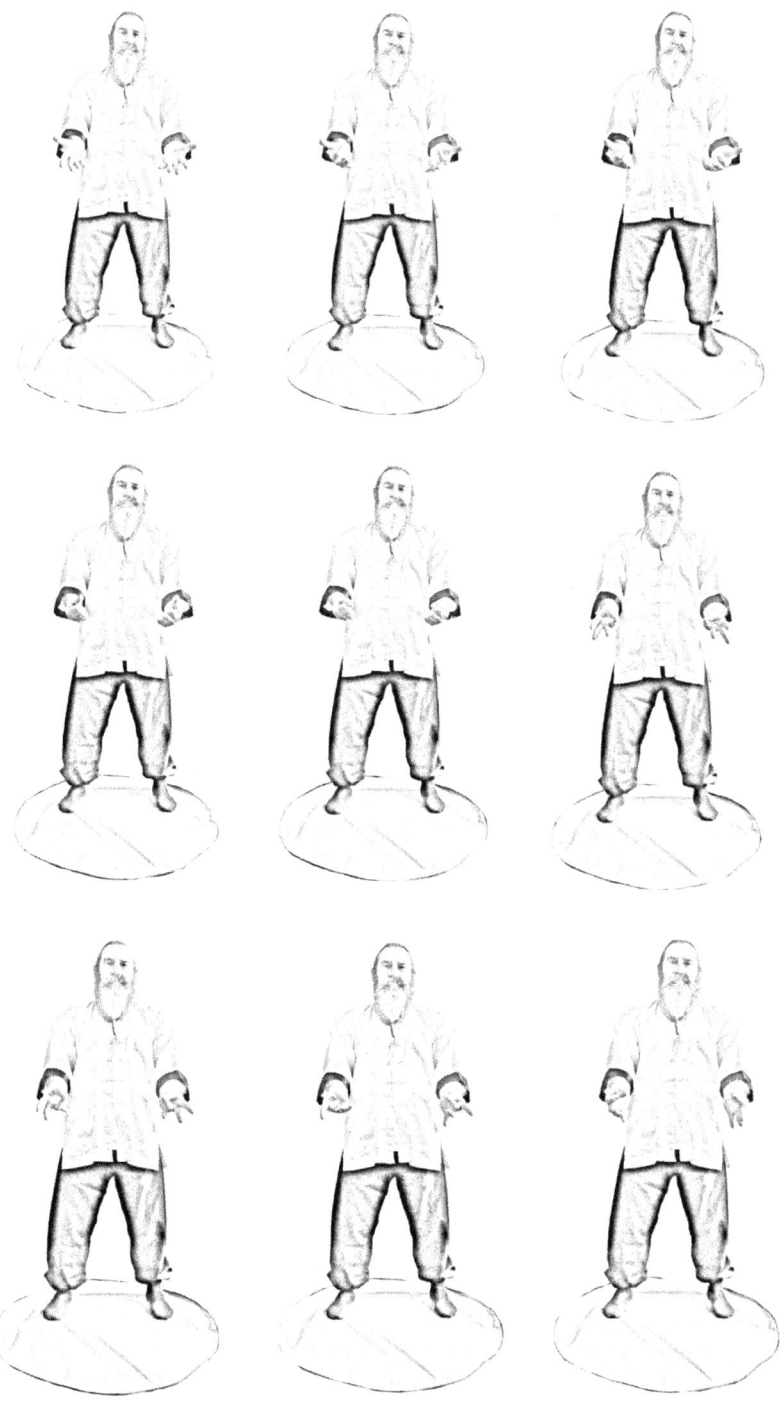

Dragon Fire Qigong

Meditations Harmony and Balanced Stretching

Dragon Fire Qigong

Meditations Harmony and Balanced Stretching

Warm the body procedure

1st page is open to connect mind, Spirit to body Kua. Move the feet to form the stand at the ready posture, with synchronicity of hand, body, feet movements. This is done to produce the activity of movement in a smooth flow.

2nd page is hands behind small of back (Ming Men), to move through the hips, Kua and waist, to warm the middle body in a smooth flow. Done 3-6 times one way then reversed.

3rd page is hands on hips to rise up and down on toes and heels, do 3-6 times, then begin to move through the waist with hands gliding diagonally upwards towards the liver or spleen, from iliac crest- warming energy into the Dai Mai belt channel and connecting smooth flowing energy through the lower body core.

4th page is from diagonal movements, completing 3-6 circulations i.e Right then left is one completion. Then begin to rise from Xia, up through the hands above the head, then press gently downwards through the central core.

5th page is with hands rising upwards to press down through the core, do so from above the head and then from the chest region. This draws energy Qi up and down connecting through the feet also, pressed into Xia. Followed by clenching fists in a hand grab, to pull in towards body Kua.

6th page is the continue to pull fist grabs into body Kua, moving up the core and down through central core, creating toning strength in hands. Followed by drawing fingers into a fist to warm the joints and hands, first with little fingers, then after 3-6 index fingers inwards. Make into a gentle fist, squeeze.

7th page is from forming fingers into fists, squeeze. Touch finger tips to thumbs 3* each upwards from little finger then downwards from index fingers. Dexterity and coordination of fingers.

8th page is shake fingers and hands as you rise up. To then squat and pull arms downwards like turbulence in movement forms. From this 3* move to circle hands and arms up and around inside to out. 3*

9th page is return to bring hands-arms outside to inside, arms not crossing as before. 3*

10th page is the completion of the circling back inside to the settle once again with diagonal, 'Dai Mai' smooth movements into rest.

Guiding Mindfelt Energy:

Guiding energy with the mind, is felt intrinsically through every aspect of Qigong, once one has tuned into the delivery of this energy. To separate its functional abilities within, one must recognise the difference in movement energies, such as dynamic implementation or fulfilling specific needs. Healing from a stationary or seated meditative form of energy, is tailored to specific requirements. Movements energy, from a mindful perspective aligns more closely with the macrocosmic element of our human form, and mastering these forms goes beyond mere awareness in one's initial stages. Understanding the potential benefits of mind-body synergy, through performance and guidance becomes internalised.

In "Guiding Energy," using Nei gong still forms in meditation, provides the mind with the optimal opportunity to develop and direct energy where it is needed most. Mind and energy merge to intuitively respond to needs, unlocking the deeper faculties of the human mind to access intent, intuition, and visualisation to guide energy. Visualisation involves using the minds eye, to perceive energy as luminous light and applying intent to direct it. Whether one is consciously aware that energy constantly flows in and out of the body and that everything emits energy or light from within, or when focusing the mind on this fact (visualising light energy), energy will respond to intent, potentially allowing for control.

One effective method is to achieve a state of meditative calm by balancing body, mind, and breath, and visualise bright, luminous white energy, descending from the Baihui centre, an energy gate, into the body through the Chong-Mai, filling the Wellness Centre Xia with vibrant, healthy energy on the inhale. Upon exhale, the energy rises upward and exits through the same channel. This visualisation technique can be practiced regularly and expanded to include other energy gates such as pressing Laogong, Yongquan, and Shang (upper Wellness Centre). It is also used in Dragon Fire Reiki fusion.

Practicing this type of visualisation technique, cultivates a mindful intent to command the flow of internal energy and can be integrated into various visualisation practices, such as toning, colour healing, or directing healing energy into organs or body parts, to enhance internal wellness.

Guided imagery, a more precise form of visualisation, targets specific effects such as healing injuries, clearing negative energy from organs, enhancing sexual potency, or safeguarding one's spiritual vitality from external negative influences. Recognise dark energy in its forms and then block or removing it.

Chapter 2: How to Find the Qi

1. Categories of Qi then Blood

To look at Qi

Qi, once formed, in the sense of our living matter being, can be understood as performing to many types or functions, specific for each activity. Comprised within the energy of Qi, which can accumulate or transform. It's purpose then, can be said to open up at least five major functions related to activity, these being directly responsible for the integrity of any entity, and the changes it undergoes.

Qi forms within a source, an opportunity of movement and growth and accompanies within these functions. Movements; in its broadest sense such as: walking, jogging, skipping; along with involuntary movements (such as breathe and heartbeat), willed actions (like feeding and speech), and mental actions (such as thought, enjoyment, and dreaming), as well as development, growth, and the life sequence (birth, maturation, and aging) - all these movements are accompanied by Qi. When viewed as in say a Reiki system (universal white light); this Qi in our Qigong; becomes an element that can infuse and exude properties, beyond the basic level. Forming new energy structures, through which to instigate a development from these very same movements or activity; known as natural energy formulations, created within a complex organism as will be developed.

Therefore, **Qi** isn't the cause of movement; rather, all things include Qi within them. As stated, the four movements in our human form derive from Ascending, Descending, Entering, and Exiting elements of movement, harmonious to the living body's presence. Inactivity, in the case of stagnancy, or loss of prevailing harmonies, fitness, mind illness, lethargy; will of course, be a cause of disharmony.

Qi in this sense of healing connection to wellness and vitality, create this opportunity of also serving to protect the body, by resisting the entry of pathological environmental agents, in TCM called 'External Pernicious Influences', and helps with combating them if they do penetrate.

Lastly, **Qi** ensures stability and governs retention, maintaining the structure and integrity of human life. Each organ has its own Qi resonance, which harmonises with the element of harmony and balance 'Five Element Theory' and the many parts that contribute to the whole or oneness needed to maintain wellness. Thus, it can help keep organs in order or place and in harmony with all others.

Qi infused with Qigong also helps with warming the Blood. Qigong elemental forms are derived for the purpose of maintaining harmony in our body, create the necessary conditions for warming body, limbs, organs, and with infusing vitality within.

Below are an example of the main five functions of **Qi** types. However; these five are 'especially important', as each associates with particular actions or specific parts of the human body.

Organ Qi: Every organ is conceived as having its own transformational Qi, like a battery, whose activity is characterised within that organs Jing. When one speaks of Heart Qi, Liver Qi or Lung Qi, the texture of Qi is the same, but its activity differs depending on that organs purpose and presence.

Meridian Qi: Meridians are a unique and critical part of TCM theory. They are the energy pathways through which Qi flows among the vital organs, through our 12 Earthly Branches or roots; to our 10 Heavenly Branches and various bodily constructs, adjusting and harmonising their activities. Qi which flows in this comprehensive network is called Meridian Qi.

Nutritive Qi (ying-qi) This Qi in 'Dragon Fire, is part of the "Nurturing Mother" host or nutrient enriching food of the soul' it is intimately connected with the Blood, manifests from the Spleen's nutritive enhancement of Blood; enriched passes through the Lungs and is absorbed into the Blood. It becomes a pulsating oxygenation of Qi throughout the human body, enriching into our blood vessels, essentials for bodily nourishment. The "Yellow Tiger" pathway of Dragon Fire.

Protective Qi (Wei-qi) This Qi is integral for the body's defence system, against harmful pathogens 'virus-colds-flus' and protects through the close surface of skin and muscles, like an armour. Wei Qi is more Yang, than Gu Qi (food Qi) their partnership of forming Nutritive Qi, is part of a delivery of Qi energies formed within Zong Qi, it is sent out to warm and nourish the body. Thus Wei Qi feeds the exterior and subcutaneous regions, in support of nourishing skin and muscles in defence of, any exogenous pathogenic factors. This Qi regulates sweat glands and pores and moistens and protects the skin and hair.

Qi of the Chest or Ancestral Qi (zong-qi) This Qi gathers in the chest, forming 'an upper sea of Qi.' Zong Qi fused by breath and food enriched in the blood delivers and collects in the chest, exits through the throat, connects with the heart and vessels, and aids in respiration. Its main function is to aid and regulate the rhythmic movement, of respiration and heartbeat, with the Lungs and Heart. The relative strength- harmony can be heard and felt in the voice, heartbeat, and pulse, all related to the Qi of the Chest.

Qi in Deficiency

Deficient Qi: In reference to disharmony, within the person from a disfunction within the 'Five Element' system or any part within this. This deficiency leads to an overall affect of lethargy or exhaustion, lack of desire to accomplish, for that matter do almost anything when an organ is depleted or unable to do its function.

Collapsed Qi: As a subcategory in 'Deficient Qi', this implies Qi is so insufficient that organs can no longer perform in its place. Then collapsed Qi, can reveal such disorders; as a prolapse of the uterus or haemorrhoids, results; loss of motivation or commitment. Among a variety of physical and emotional conditions, those thought to diminish your Qi. Are the causes from chronic stress and sleep deprivation. Both of which elevate the stress hormone cortisol, interfering with immune function and increases the risk of depression and burnout.

Stagnant Qi: This is another broad category of Qi disharmony. In this disharmony, the normal movement of Qi is impaired, blocked, does not flow through the body as it should. Stagnant Qi therefore, can also lead to impairment of an Organ, or the status quo of transfer. Stagnant Qi in the Liver for instance, may result in abdominal distension, moodiness, or a sense of deep frustration leading to anger.

Rebellious Qi: This particular form of Stagnant Qi, has the implication that Qi moves in the wrong direction. Rebellious Qi is in a sense, a pathological response such as; in the Chong Mai where Qi becomes unregulated. Emotional stress suppressed, or Blood/Kidney deficiency in the vessel or within the lower abdomen. As this manifests fundamental disharmony, and as described through the Yin/Yang spectrum, harmony needs Organ meridian platforms, to be inducive to good balance. The ideal balance is needed, for instance, the Stomach needs its energy focus to be downwards. If upset, it will rise upwards to the Spleen, disrupting their harmonious flow. Vomiting or nausea may occur correcting this imbalance. Or vice a versa, disharmony of the Spleen may induce diarrhoea.

Deficient Qi: Yin condition, a depletion characterised by under-activity, while **Stagnant Qi** is a Yang condition, associated with excessiveness.

To look at Blood

Jin-Ye (Body Fluids)
These are the liquids that help protect, nourish, and lubricate your body. They include perspiration, tears, saliva, stomach acid, mucus, semen, breast milk, and other bodily secretions.

The Jin are the lighter, purer fluids that moisten and nourish the skin and muscles.
The Ye are the darker, denser fluids; they nourish the internal organs, brain, bones, and body orifices.

Blood (xue)

This would be deemed the most important fluid of the body, as in TCM principles; blood is the foundational element towards the formation of our bones, nerves, skin, muscles and organs. Generic sense; the fundamental quality of human life, nourishing the body, moistening body tissues, and likened to the sense of a cosmos, an all-pervasive Qi. Blood also contains the Shen, or Spirit of our soul breath and vitality; in its delivery it balances the psyche, is a responsive, accepting, effortless, soft, and nurturing complement. Qi and Blood are the Yin and Yang of life activity. Qi embodies effort, Blood is effortless. Qi quickens, Blood softens. Qi activates, Blood relaxes. Qi is tense and tight; Blood is smooth and languid. Qi is becoming, Blood is being.

Origins of Blood: Blood originates through the mastication of food. After being received into the Stomach, this food is 'ripened'. Spleen distills and purifies this essence before transporting upwards into the Lungs. During the upward movement, Nutritive Qi begins to turn the essence into enriched Blood. This change is completed when the essence reaches the Lungs, where the now transformed food combines with the portion of air described as 'clear'; Oxygenation. This combines within the union of rising Kidney Qi, which finally produces this clean, oxygenated, nutritious Blood. The Blood is then propelled through the body by the Heart Qi in coordination with the Qi of the Chest. Another element of Blood production is through the forging of inner cauldron energy - "Marrow- Xi Sui Jing."
    This combination of Qi activity, the base transmutation of Blood within the body's elements, forged from marrow out. Blood, along with the Liver, Spleen, and Kidneys of the Five Element Theory, connects the system and the Marrow.

Relationships of Blood

These three Organs in our body: Heart, Liver, and Spleen, have a special relationship with our Blood. Blood depends on the heartbeat for its harmonious, smooth, and continuous circulation, back and forth. This in TCM states that 'the Heart rules the Blood'.

An inactive body will create less heart pulse, or need for Blood than an active one. Thus, inactivity provides a need for the storage of Blood. The Liver; then stores while cleaning Blood.
    This filtration method is used as a holistic approach to regulate, the design for overall wellness. Knowing the Spleen is

regarded as the nutritional supply of substance 'nourish in' gleaned from the Stomach, it also supplements a healthy Blood supply.

Disharmonies of Blood

Two major categories of Blood disharmony are Deficient Blood and Congealed Blood. Deficient Blood reveals a pattern of insufficiency in Blood supply, to the whole body system or part (Organ, Limb), results in a disharmony occurring. Symptoms of this may include pale skin, lustreless face, dizziness, tight muscles, restlessness, and dry skin.

Psychologically, Blood disharmony can lead to low self-esteem, lack of self-worth, or even poor memory.

Congealed Blood means that Blood is not flowing smoothly, having become obstructed in some way, causing an accumulation of disharmonious energy. This condition can be characterised by sharp pain, stabbing pains, tumours, cysts, or swelling of the organs. On a psychological level, there may be an inability to feel safe or feeling timid, along with an overwhelm toward excessive vigilance. Creating Mental health issues; Suspiciousness, paranoid ideation, and delusions can also be associated with Congealed blood.

Essence (jing)

Essence, the translation of the Chinese word Jing, is the texture specific to organic life. Jing governs your reproduction and regeneration. This Vital life force- energy, forms the fundaments of being. It's the substance that makes living beings unique and distinct from inorganic things. So and according to TCM theory, Jing or Essence summarised here in two parts: Yin, being congenital or pre- natal is a kind of intrinsic, soft, and juicy potential, for inherent living things, formed to become life cycles. Forged in us, from the fathers sperm- into fertilisation of a mothers ovum. Grown within the Mother host from a pre- designed limitation, this pre- disposition will be inherent, throughout a persons life time.

Post- natal Jing is acquired after birth, through food, water, oxygen and is benefited further, by environmental circumstances. This is regarded as the Yang form of Jing.

Transformations of Essence 'Yin and Yang' Jing, transform and create or replenish each other, the yang energy circulates through the eight extraordinary vessels "Qi Jing Ba Mai" and transform to become and replenish Yin; in turn Marrow becomes blood, body fluid and semen. The quality of this essence or texture, that imbues an organism with the possibility of development, from conception

to death. It's also responsible for the development of our deepest awareness and wisdom.
Disharmonies of Essence could develop an improper maturation, sexual dysfunction, with inability to reproduce, along with detrimental aging, within this, the incapacity to be self-reflective as a person matures.

Qi and Essence both have to do with movement. Qi and Essence in an individual's moment, have to do with the dynamics of pre-ordained supply (genetics) or disposition of spirit- self in spite of delivery. Essence is Yin and Qi is Yang; when compared to Blood, Essence however; is the more active, or Yang phenomenon. Blood is associated with the everyday cyclical process of maintenance, nourishment, and repair. Therefore, in relation to Blood, Essence is Yang; in relation to Essence, Blood is Yin.

Spirit (shen)

Spirit, translated into Chinese as Shen, Po, Hun etc; {Hun is the ethereal soul; (Liver) it is regarded as the imprint of self, that which remains after cessation of life. Po; is the portion of a persons spirit, that absolutely is dependant on the physical life. (Corporal Soul Lung) When breath ceases, the Po begins to disintegrate.} These are some of the fundamental textures of Shen unique to human life. In the same way that Essence (jing) distinguishes organic life from inorganic material, Spirit separates human life from animal life.
    While the Chinese system has taught me that in their minds, the sense of spirit is in the so called flesh connect realm, as in they are all focused upon the sense of a persons body, energy is developed to derive purpose or moment! But, does not necessarily mean an existence, is still propagated to install, in a self form- Spirit being.
    More to the line of as in living matter, spirit in the person, has traits that reveal propagations on instilled or collected into as human ideals, in this they may believe animals share instinctive drives, reactivity, and various emotions with humans, yet in TCM mind, only humans are thought to possess true Spirit.

The Spirit, I reflect in Dragon Fire - or, for that matter, in "Dragon Fire Soul Breath" - is indifference. The Spirit in 'Dragon Fire' represents the collection of inherited responses that can accumulate through the perspective of the beastly manners inherent, becoming noticeable to reflections and awareness.

An individual may show spirit in the sense of commitment, kindness, loving heart, etc. Beastly attributes that this animal kingdom, also entails.

Meditations Harmony and Balanced Stretching

There are good and bad attributes in individual circumstances, in humankind, as well as in the animal kingdom. The Spirit in my "Dragon Fire Soul Breath" represents the unique Self in Spirit form. It is, and has now become entwined in human form, within this embodiment of the living matter's realm. It therefore attributes itself as a Spirit form firstly, and then a 'Living Soul' breath secondly. Therefore, in 'Dragon Fire' I see my Spirit itself, in its true form 'pure white transparent' seperate from; the light energy of this universe, and not tied only to this worlds ideals.

Attributes of living matter can be obtained in this element of inheritance of biological structure, yet Spirit, in its true form, exists differentially only as an attachment, not as a whole. Therefore, a Spirit, although in this now; could already exist separate from the conclusions of interference of bodily function, even to the extent of beastly connotations of shown traits. Of niceness, or badness, that can become upon an individual.

This Spirit identity; then leads a seperate vision of being, as I have seen throughout my lifetime, and my journey as humankind into the dilemmas of conflict. Constant in this world are these indifferences, that a soul complying to self, if one does not fit the criteria, for instance, of being the same in spirit, whether through possession from one identity to another, as in culture, religion, or even the sense of accumulated decency. Then Spirit also becomes that which is in need of training, back to or away from certain perspectives in the living matter realm, of this, our humankind's endeavours.

This is the construct of my search through the partnership of Dragon Fire: Qigong-Nei gong- Nei dan gong and, of course, why I have created my own form of "Chi Boxing; Qigong." Dragon Fire Soul Defence! It is also the prevailing element of my discovery that these above-mentioned things exist, as to allow oneself "such as I am" to become involved with my own interpretations of living worth. Both in the sense of Soul breath, in self-discovery and inclusive to the way or Dao. That is inclusive to finding a sense of becoming self-harmony, in this living matter realm. That of which truly is an environment of absolute "evils" presence, had set upon my living, loving, Spirit-mind, and Will (Yi). This to me, does not imply entirely to all people, as their unique self may differ, as a part of another! It does signify that my own perceptions of spirit are different, from the so called TCM of Chinese culture, or for that matter religious personifications.

    This, my spirit sense connect- has shown that to me; as an energy- my Qigong practice also created within me, glowing bright white spirit energy as well, I can see this when I practice my forms. This difference is noticeable to me, in the texture of first seeing myself in spirit form as a child, as to when I see the white energy of myself, now in living energy Qigong performed.

3. ***The 3 treasures***

Just as the earth contains air, water, and land, the basic substances of your body are Qi, Body Fluids (Jin-Ye), Essence (Jing), Blood (Xue), and Spirit (Shen). These five vital substances circulate through your meridians and body, linking your whole being. When flowing smoothly, they contribute to your healthy state, but when blocked or deficient, they may form symptoms like; aches, tension, swelling, asthma, indigestion, and fatigue. The most important of these five vital substances are; Shen, Qi, and Jing. Together, they are called the Three Treasures (sānbǎo). Qigong specifically focuses on cultivating these three treasures.

These **"Three Treasures"** can be described into our context of **Qigong** as these.

Table of The Three Treasures

Lower Treasure	Middle Treasure	Upper Treasure
Physical	Emotional	Mental
Earth	Self	Heaven
Body	Breath	Mind
Martial	Health	Spiritual
Jing	Qi	Shen
Lower Wellness Centre (Xia)	Middle Wellness Centre (Zhong)	Upper Wellness Centre (Shang)
1st Wei Qi Field	2nd Wei Qi Field	3rd Wei Qi Field

4. ***Jing-Qi-Shen***

Three Treasures in connection to: Jing, Qi, Shen.

	Jing	Qi	Shen
Energy	Sexual	Life-Breath	Spirit -Self
Organ	Kidney-Lungs	Spleen-Liver	Heart
Element	Water	Air	Fire
Movement	Down	Down-Up	Up
Wellness Centre	Lower (Xia)	Middle (Zhong)	Upper (Shang)
Circulatory System	Marrow (Bones)	Meridians	Extra Meridians

5. Categories of Qi:

- **Breathe Qi** – (Zong QI) from respiration.
- **Food Qi** – (Gu Qi) from diet.
- **Original Qi** – (Yuan Qi) inherited from parents or the universe.
- **Internal Qi** – Meridians Qi inside the body.
- **External Qi** – (Shen Yi) emanating from the body.
- **Nutritive Qi** – (Ying Qi) flows inside.
- **Protective Qi** – (Wei Qi) energetic barrier against pathogens and/or negative influences.

Three Treasures:

Metaphorically, the "Three Treasures" are like the three planes of being in one: a physical body, an emotional connection, and a mental connection. These "Three Treasures" can be described in the context of Qigong as follows:

Qi comes from Jing; Jing depends on Qi.

When Qi is active, Shen appears.

When Shen is weak, it lacks Jing and Qi.

- **Wei Qi fields** are the energy spectrum surrounding the body's aura, encasing it in an external protective barrier. They connect through the energy formed in the Three Wellness Centres (Xia, Zhong, Shang). "Wei," meaning "external," propels outward, increasing in thickness from the first to the third energy centre:
    1. The first is an auric energy closest to the body.
    2. The second is an auric energy connecting through the heart-emotions (Xin).
    3. The third is when the auric fields have extended into a large elliptical orb, surrounding the presence of Spirit/Self. (Shen- Yi)

Chapter 3: Context of Five Elements- Dragon Fire Qigong

1. ***Qualities of the 5 elements***

Connection and Interaction in a Theory

In Dragon Fire Qigong the theory of Five Elements-phases; is the discovery that in order to exist as living beings, we became this harmonised fluctuation of a system formed, to create, a fulfilment and generation of energy.

Along with this the need (us being formed- life), also is a need to control or control within this living energy, in some way that is balanced harmony.

This structure of the 'five', shows how we were in a natural state of balance within nature, and as a philosophy; all things within the construct of being created, can follow a pathway of general knowledge, principled; to establish a better understanding and awareness of ourselves. It also reveals that the balance of all things have a play; prewritten, within our capability to construct our thoughts, and our pathways, along this journey within life, nature, or the many things.
 So as we analyse the principles of awareness (us within nature) established, we begin to see the patterns that will always be this establishment, of the five elements or phases. Having now understood that our very make up in general awareness, follows a pathway to these connections- fulfil.

Realising then, such things as seasons of life; winter, summer, spring etc exist in harmonies of natural energy, as an environment succeeds. So too does the development of our generation, birth, youth, aged and passing.

So within Qigong 'Dragon Fire' is the platform of lifes harmony, established to promote a better, natural balance of harmonious connection within ourselves and the natural environment.

What could 'Five Element theory' show to us? It could show us about this world of which we now live? First, it reveals to us; about how all things are connected and/or within each element, how they are relating. Let's take as an example, the Water element. So, when looking at the 'Five Elements' table:

Water relates to winter, a cold climate, the north (as a natural energy, water sinks), the colours are represented in 'Dragon Fire' as dark-blue/black.

Kidneys, in the 'negative energy sensed', are interconnected by the emotion of fear/fright. These things which share a deep, and somewhat invisible connection to each other. As when in winter, we feel a cold essence; it will relate upon and impact in some way upon our Kidneys; the emotion 'fear' is linked too; as a frozen chill sensed, interacting, and not always obvious, or visible.

These 'Five Elements' reveal to us, how the organs and bodily systems, in which our pathways are already connecting, within a balanced harmony, to each other and all bodily functions; and how we are connected to our environment? The natural world; or how our world, is part of a greater universe.

Many of us today as a people; would have lost this deep connection in nature, that our ancestors had to have had installed naturally, and now no longer are able to easily feel this oneness or truth resonate in our conscious being. This Universal principle of oneness in connection, still must exist nonetheless.

The Balancing Relationships of Generation and Control

Having mentioned previously about Generation and Control aspects, we in Qigong and 'Dragon Fire' connect the construct of these into our knowledge base. Five Elements; like phases, are the fundamental properties of nature in motion. As there is balance within this dynamism; their performance does not become a static sensed energy, as they naturally need to fluctuate between their needs to also fulfil harmony and balance.

This is a template for (Traditional Chinese medicine) and part of our formulations with Qigong? As the principle of 'Generate and Control' become better understood, we then become knowing about the construct of energy "Yin and Yang." And, the variations within the performance of our natural ability, to promote this into our life energy.

When we speak about the Five Elements-phases of generation, it means a relationship that nurtures and promotes growth. Often taught as a mother- child construct. The mother gives birth to a child, providing nurturing energy of support, this ensures the growth of that child. So as an example; in the generate life sequence, we can talk about the relationship with {Kidneys and Liver harmony}. Water supports Wood, as does (Kidneys support the liver function).

Control, in terms of the Five Elements, represents a relationship that acts as a restraining energy or force, making sure that things do not grow too quickly or too slowly, neither too strong nor too weak. Without this type of support; things could become unhealthy, fall out of proportion; balance would be lost! This construct of delivery then; is as such a directive for your life pathway and awareness training, into Qigongs living harmony.

As a sense of the type of connections of which we speak of, in Qigong, these 'five element organs' along with their supply of life Qi, energy and wellness producing harmonies.

Is described below to reveal in one of the characteristics, of a vital body organs roll within uniformity of purpose, within the concept of this enforcing 'Five Element Theory'; and as a holistic sense of this systems measure.

Liver/Gallbladder: According to Five Element Theory

The Wood Element

The Wood element; like the seed of a tree sprouts upwards through the ground toward the Sun, and at the same time grows downwards into the earth. Its form grows in every direction and exhibits the fundamental elements; those- Entering, Exiting, Ascending and Descending. Its ability to move with and bend to such force as a wind rather than break, means you have the ability to adapt. As will be described; the Liver according to the principles of (Traditional Chinese Medicine) is the organ responsible for our smooth flow of emotions, as well as our Qi and blood. It being the organ that is most affected through excessive stress or emotions.

The Liver's partner organ is the Gallbladder. Its Genetic aspiration: evolution via growth and adaption connects through the Spirit property of Hun: (Ethereal-Soul).

- The livers responsibility of blood storage and its connection to the needs of our body feeding (return to spirit), create a smooth flow of Qi and blood harmony, naturally throughout our body system. Connects to the sense of emotive 'Physiology' has a direct influence to our performing to balanced, harmony.
- As the sensory organ the eyes, are directly related to the liver. We can look to the disharmony of our liver system, when issues occur such as; blurry vision, sore eyes, red or dry eyes, itchy eyes; it may be a signal that your Liver is not functioning smoothly.
- Tendons, as being the tissue associated with the Liver. As in (TCM) state that strength comes from the tendons, not muscles. An expression of directive would lead to; be more like a cat that is strong, agile, and flexible, tendon strength.
- Sour taste corresponds to Liver. If you crave sour foods, that may be your Liver communicating that it needs an extra boost, inclusion of sweet and sour recipes in your diet is a (TCM).
- As with in 'Anger' this emotion associates with the Liver, often opens up to irritability, getting angry easily, or have trouble unwinding from your day's activities. If you have trouble reasoning or going with the flow and letting things

Meditations Harmony and Balanced Stretching

go, you are experiencing a Liver function disharmony. Whilst experiencing these emotions chronically or excessively, can unbalance your livers function. Remember, when in harmony positive emotions such as: Benevolence and Humour abide.

You can use basic guidelines like these to begin Qigong awareness, grow to understand what each of our organs may be asking for in support. In this case use these 'signs' to rebalance yourself, when finding your inner self- balanced and in harmony, fulfil your own ability to participate by performing your own energy based qigong, within your own practice, fulfilling a living life pathway.

Simple Tips for Everyday Liver Health: If your Wood element is healthy, you will feel the sense of being present, with ability to visualise your future, make sensible decisions, see better whilst remaining subtle and flexible. Be more capable and confident as you express through your abilities in a creative way. Remember to:

- Stay calm, don't get caught up in the sense of a spring's intensity or new energies! Take things more easily, relax as you go slow; take walks in the park or do other gentle exercises . Those that relax your mind, body, and spirit. Let go of those stressful situations if you can, but if that's not possible, use some of the stress-relieving tips below.
- The use of a tapping massage technique, this form of energy fusion, tapping your legs up and down from inside of your thighs and calves, starting at the ankles, this gently stimulates your Liver meridian, allows your qi to flow more freely and relaxes your Liver energy.
- Avoid alcohol! We all know that our Liver is responsible for the metabolising of alcohol. Therefore, drinking in moderation is a benefit toward preserving your Liver's energy and giving it a break.
- Remember to engage in gentle exercise, such as swimming or walking, instead of the hard and fast exercises of our youth, that overwork or overstretch. Tendons, when overworked eventually lose their flexibility, impacting the Liver function of being "flexible." Qigong is perfect!

Some of these principal 'Dynamic Qigong and Nei gong' platforms such as- Vital Body Qi Wash-Wood, in this book are designed for the purpose of relaying this intent to harmonise 'Vital' organ balance.

"Dragon Fire Qigong; Dynamic Qigong", are very suitable for providing the essence of liver restoration and for developing wellness healing or vitality.

2. Peak periods of visceral qi

In the context of Dragon Fire Qigong, visceral feelings refer to those deeply felt sensations, being that they are challenging to control or disregard, and they arise independently of conscious thought. They encompass a profound sense of joy in simply being alive. Visceral feelings are governed by a system of interconnected neural structures in the brain, which play a role in regulating emotional behaviour.

Peak Periods of Visceral Qi:

Time	Organ	Element	Healing-sound
11pm-1am	Gallbladder	Wood	Shuu
1am-3am	Liver	Wood	Shuu
3am-5am	Lung	Metal	Ahhh
5am-7am	Large intestine	Metal	Ahhh
7am-9am	Stomach	Earth	Whoo
9am-11am	Spleen	Earth	Whoo
11am-1pm	Heart	Fire	Haaa
1pm-3pm	Small intestine	Fire	Haaa
3pm-5pm	Bladder	Water	Chruee
5pm-7pm	Kidney	Water	Chruee
7pm-9pm	Pericardium	Air	Shee
9pm-11pm	Triple burner	Air	Shee

3. 5 element cycles

Five Elements Cycle: Once one understands the relationship between our mind and intention, they are ready to identify a purpose in their practice, of creating an environment that supports it. In our Qigong for health, participants are asked to visualise these kinds of vivid scenarios, movements of Qi, around and through the body, in using colours, sensed emotions, organs, sensations, sounds, and more. These are interwoven into complete cycles in the formulation of Qi energies, performing functions to our senses of wellness, restoration, recovery, mindfulness, and joyous being.

Meditations Harmony and Balanced Stretching

This purpose is to visualise the formation of sensing Qi flow through organs, meridians, or energy centres, as has been stated, the "Five elements" embody several meanings that can be applied according to one's needs.

Each element is a direct embodiment of the concept it represents. Fire, for example, embodies heat and rising energy. When looking at the Five elements table, it represents the Heart, which houses the spirit, the virtue of Love, and the acquired emotion of over-excitement. It also symbolises Summer, the colour Red, and in the Circle of Five actions (martial form), it is P'ao (Fire).

4. *5 elemental properties*

The Five Elemental Properties*

Earth: Earth corresponds to the Spleen (Yin organ) and Stomach (Yang organ). When in a balanced state, it is expressed as the virtue of Trust and Faith. The emotion of Worry can be the negative element that affects the Spleen and can be sensed in the pit of one's stomach in certain scenarios.

The Earth element is related to sweet tastes {not sweet sugar, but soft brown rice sweet or sweet potato} and is represented by a yellow/brown colour.

The resonating sound for Earth is Whoo and is activated by "singing." In the body, it is reflected by the quality of the mouth and muscles. In terms of seasons, it is regarded as the centre, like the grounding period between each season, a time of transition from one to another. Earth is the centre of all directions. The qualities of Earth are "grounding, nourishing, and nurturing."

Metal: Metal corresponds to the Lungs (Yin organ) and Large Intestine (Yang organ). When in a balanced state, it is expressed as the 'Virtue of Integrity' and the ability to let go of attachments. The emotions of grief or sorrow are reflective of the Metal element. Its colour is White for purity and is activated by the resonating sound AAHH. In the body, it is reflected in the skin, hair, nose, and through the action of crying.

A healthy Metal element allows one to feel in harmony with this universe, with an appreciation of a valued self, within your own space. Knowing that there is a connection to everything of value outside your boundaries, yet keeping to a capacity to change and still remain in harmony, within yourself. It relates to the season of Autumn and is the West direction in the compass form.

Foods associated with Metal have a pungent taste, and qualities of Metal are sharp, focused, determined, and persistent. Energy of

Metal is "contracting." Metal element forms and connects your earthly boundaries, through your first breath, until your last breath.

Water: Water corresponds to the Kidneys (Yin organ) and Urinary Bladder (Yang organ). When in a balanced state, it is expressed as 'Virtue of Wisdom' and the ability for confidence and courage. The Emotion of Fear, including that of uncertainty, of being, or doing, and having enough! - Drains the Kidneys and consumes water reserves. Water is in the season of Winter; its colour is Dark-Blue-Black, which can represent the sense of deep introspection. Listening, quiet, stillness, conserving, dormancy, and the essence of Yin are its reflections, and it is activated by the resonating sound of Chruee.

The body reflects in the quality of fluids within, the strength of bones, and of hearing. It is associated with the North direction in the compass form and with foods that are salty and in all bodies of water. Energy of Water is "conserving."

Wood: Wood corresponds to the Liver (Yin organ) and Gall Bladder (Yang organ). When in a balanced state, it is expressed as the 'Virtue of Kindness' and 'Benevolence'. When out of balance, the wood element becomes rigid and inflexible, highly defensive with anger and irritation. The wood element flourishes in the Spring, and its colour is Spring green, the resonating sound is Shuu, and it is expressed by shouting. In the body, it is reflected in the quality and strength of tendons, nerves, nails, and in the eyes. It associates with the East direction in the compass form, and the flavour of its associated foods is sour. The energy of Wood is "Creative."

Fire: The Fire element corresponds to the Heart- (Yin organ) and Small intestine (Yang organ). When in a balanced state, Fire is confidence in expression, as a virtue in Unconditional Love, and the ability to offer abundance of joy. When out of balance, the Fire element becomes nervous, agitated, or over-excited, consuming itself and jumping around like a blazing fire, making it difficult to find true direction. The Fire element represents our Spirit-Self, and the heart is its home. As the Heart opens with pure loving energy, it preserves our connection to our celestial being.

Fire element is the peak of Summer, during which the heat exposes life to the maximum of Yang energies, representing the culmination of growth. The resonating sound for Fire is HAAA, and it can be expressed through laughter. In the body, it is reflected in the quality of blood, perspiration, and complexion of the skin and face. Fire is associated with the Southerly direction of our compass form and the bitter tastes of food. This is the "expanding energy" of Fire!

Chapter 4: Simple in Practice

1. ***Connecting basics to a specific need and give examples***

Simple in Practice:

Once your understanding of the principles behind the 'Five Elements Cycle' and the acquaintance within their symbolic relationships, of each element, you should begin to focus your intention onto specific areas of needed attention. When addressing these needs, remember to consider the 'Five Elements' in conjunction with the 'Three Treasures' to gain a clearer perspective on your energy work during Qigong practice.

If you intend to focus on a single aspect while working with the Five Elements? - for example, strengthening your heart or kidneys - you should maintain a singular direction of applications. If practicing the Water element, exercises such as "Three Rivers Rolling-Kidneys" Dragon Fire Qigong, or the Five Element "Vital Body Qi Wash-Water" may be beneficial.
Follow these with mindful meditations 'Fire/Water' standing meditations, or the involving visualisation of colour tones, or purging of negative energies through exhalation.

You may also choose to transition your focus from Water to another element, such as Wood, facilitating an overflow of energy that naturally supports Wood's progression. Especially if wishing to produce renewed energy say after sexual performances, or a long night. Alternatively, redirecting attention to the Fire Element can help cool down the inner fire of the Heart, through Water element meditations.

There are two fundamental transformational cycles where these energies interact and counterbalance each other to maintain homeostasis. One is the Creative or generative cycle, where each energy stimulates and amplifies the next - Water generates Wood, Wood generates Fire, and so on, completing the cycle with the creation of Water. The other is the Control or subjugation cycle, where each energy impedes and/or reduces the activity of the next in- Water impedes Fire, Fire reduces Metal, and so forth, completing with the impeding of Water.

Qigong provides a mechanism through which one can balance and/or guide, these Five Elemental energies devised within the human body system. By utilising both control and generative cycles, normal balance and natural equilibrium can be restored.

All our vital organs are paired in Yin and Yang sets, each associated with one of the 'Five Elemental Energies'. For example, the Yin

Heart and Yang Small Intestine, responsible for circulation and assimilation, are governed by Fire Energy, associated with emotions like joy and love, and the colour red. Similarly, the Yin Kidneys and Yang Urinary Bladder, governing functions such as bone health and fluid regulation, are controlled by Water, associated with emotions like fear, restraint, suppression or fright, disturbs a natural flow of harmony sensed; within positive energy, such as with the wisdom of calm, settled, affecting change and represented by the colour dark blue/black.

Specific Qigong exercises influence the energies of each vital organ system, through their respective meridians. A weak heart can be strengthened with exercises stimulating the Fire energy of the Heart, while an overactive heart, can be balanced by exercises that enhance the Water energy of the Kidneys, thereby regulating excessive Fire energy through the Water-Fire control cycle, that could culminate in a mindful Qi wash.

Similar results can be achieved by applying associated elements to stimulate or pacify various energies. For instance, the Fire energy of the heart can be amplified by wearing red clothing or softened by wearing pink, and dietary choices such as bitter flavours or herbs can influence energy dynamics. Similarly, wearing green clothing and consuming sour foods can boost the Wood energy of the Liver.

The combinations within this system are vast, allowing for experimentation with various combinations of the "Five Elements and Three Treasures." These practices are also intertwined with Feng Shui principles, to create positive energy within the home environment. Harmony of Wind and Water governance, display organised positioning, or practice. As should we deliver harmony within Qigong!

Conceptual Theory of Dragon Fire Qigong:

The theory of Dragon Fire is to cultivate an internal energy that resides within, which formulates and gathers, allowing oneself to transform, project, transfer, and combine intrinsic energy in forms and phases necessary for achieving health, wellness, and healing restoration.

Through the energy gates of Laogong and Yongquan (palms of hands and soles of feet), the practitioner begins to absorb more Qi energy. By accumulating this energy through dynamic and tranquil forms into the Wellness Centres (Xia, Zhong, and Shang), and through the Microcosmic and Macrocosmic Energy Pathways, the practitioner can begin to utilise this buildup of energies. This can extend to the hands for massaging, replacing negative energy, or simply applying it to an area for healing benefits in various ways.

The practitioner starts to feel and sense this energy form, as a type of internal strength, within the body, especially through the hands. Therefore, the hands become crucial in recognising and delivering movements and forms, whether dynamic or tranquil.

Laogong serves as a gateway through which energy can be drawn in and expelled during toning and purging exercises.

As the practitioner begins to recognise this exchange of energy, they can perform as if the mind, body, and spirit within are unified. This manifests as muscular sensing, recognition of skeletal form, and the presentation of mindful energy, which is the essence of Qigong. This completion leads to wellness, healing, mindfulness, and joyful being.

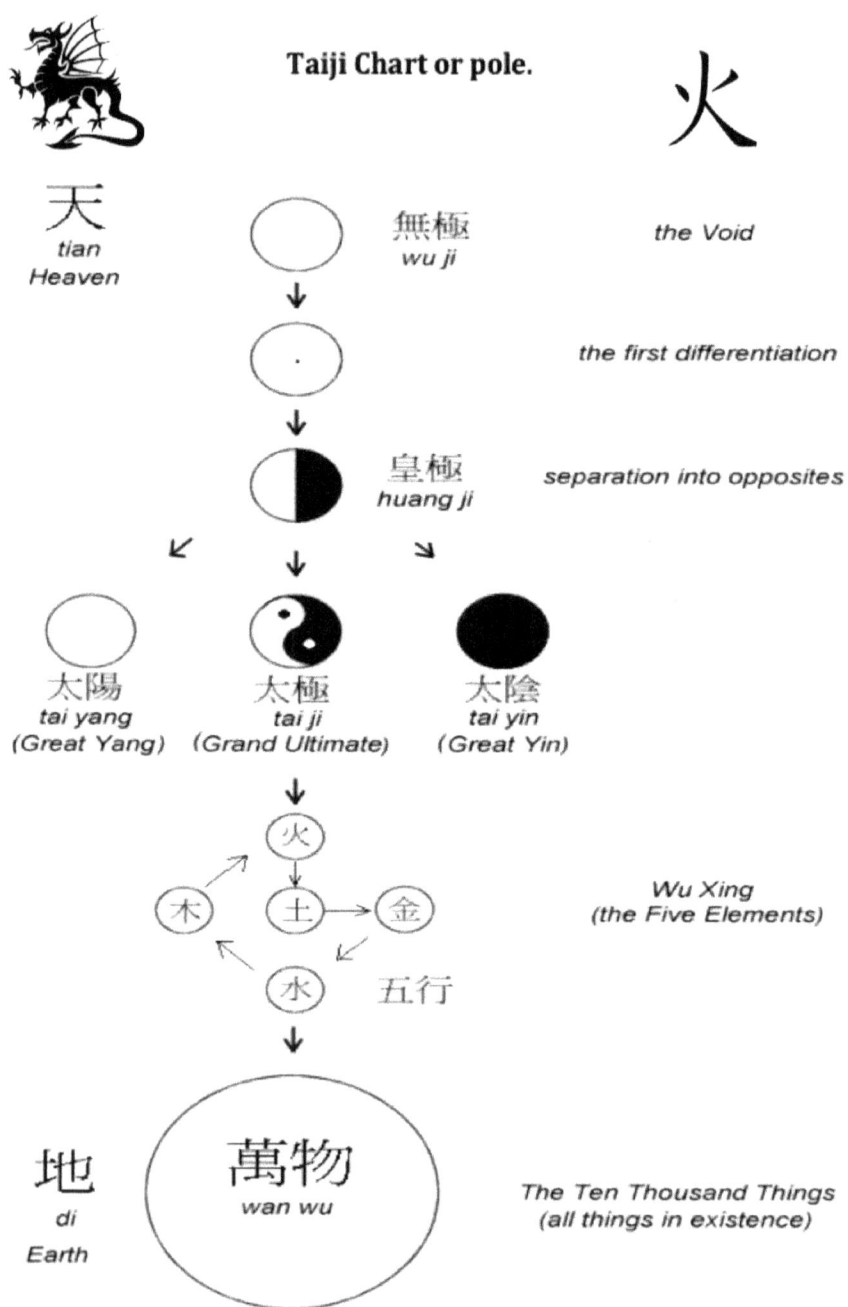

Chapter 5: Yin and Yang

Yin and Yang Theory
(Here in Connection to Traditional Chinese Medicine/TCM)

This symbol, which most people have seen in a variety of contexts, simplifies things down to one and stylish image. As far as description through a symbol goes, it just doesn't get more elementary than Yin-Yang. Yin-Yang described through human conceptual evolution, has become an incredibly complex adage to our philosophical reasonage. What Yin-Yang points to and represents is so vast it encompasses everything in this; our known Universe within a concept.

"Integral to Chinese culture through thousands of years"- Yin and Yang, like TCM's Five Element theory, and Eight Tri Grams, are the development of Chinese culture. References to Yin and Yang in some recorded histories date; thousands of years to a time even before the Yi Jing (The Book of Changes, a text style delivery of; dynamic balance within opposites and divination of unfolding events and change) based on the Eight tri grams, of which were designed well after the original construct of the broken and unbroken line signage, of this incorporation of theology system.

Yin and Yang can be distinctively revealed through Chinese perceptions, in terms of the perception, their profound elementary principles that offer up this, understanding and expression in a unique way, within viewing human kinds understandings of this world and of this greater universe. They are profoundly separated from the Western way of discovery, literally and figuratively formed as if in a world apart.

Opposite yet Complementary Energies.

Everything contains Yin and Yang. These two opposite yet complementary energies. But, what does this actually represent? Even though these two are totally different-opposite-in their individual qualities of perspective and nature, they are interdependent.

Yin and Yang cannot exist without each other; they are never separate. For example, night and day form a Yin-Yang pair. Nighttime is the Yin and the Daytime is Yang. Night looks and is very different than day, yet these things are impossible to have in context without the other. Sun light opposed to shade. Yang the sunny side of the hill, with shade to the opposite.

Both create a totality, within existing; as a complete whole. This inseparable and interpenetrative relationship, yet not explainable as always in an absolute! Is reflection in the form of the Yin-Yang symbol.

The two opposing colour dots shown within each of the two sections (represented by black and Red in Yin and Yangs first age of development) which symbolised space- cold empty black, with fusion heat as friction and as a solid matter forged from light into matter. Into the construct of polar opposites; White and Black in the modern Taiji, represents that there is always some Yang (white) within Yin (black) and vice versa. No matter where you connect within this concept and theory, of the circle of energy, each half will always contain some Yang and some Yin. Nothing it would seem is absolute, or without Yang and Yin. (Except) nothingness, the totality of end, or totality of eternity- eternal spirit light.

Balance and Harmony

In the Chinese Taiji Yin-Yang symbol, Yin represented by (the black) contains a partnership of Yang (in the form of a white dot). There is Yin, decisively held within a Yang energy. Resulting because within all things of this physical universe, Yin energy must still contain some Yang.

This revelation in- such as; Yin can transform into Yang under certain conditions? Heated water would rise up as steam, or evaporate up into the atmosphere, yet return once more into its Yin essence as a solid; as does rain fall from a cloud formed into this state, water would then eventually fall. This occurs because Yang is always present in concept with Yin. So there is this balance of, or connection in a way that goes beyond just balance, to one of balanced harmony. When two things are balanced, they can seem equal, yet still be separate. In a relationship of harmony? Two energies blend into one wholeness, as is a perfect embodiment of this established image Yin-Yang symbol.

Structurally Yin -Yang reveals this dynamism, yet with a flowing intimacy happening, automatic and continuous, creating balance and rebalance. In the natural world; this phenomenon is revealed in construct, as within the changing of seasons: as mentioned in the 'Five elements-phases'; warmth of spring and summer heat, gradually turns cool in autumn to become winter cold, as does winter yield to the warmth of spring again. A perpetuating circle of influences. Seen also within this as a perpetuating Yang and Yin development, a working balance.

In terms of (TCM) and our personal health, think of how you feel when well, you might not think of; I am concerned about being unhealthy, for that matter! Your life, may just be flowing and moving happily- balanced and in harmony. Your life, (heart-mind-emotions, and spirit Xin) of which can also be acceptably harmonised, progressing along a pathway within your life. This is precisely the state through TCM- Qigong we seek to create; your understanding of healthy balance. Fundamental Qigong theories therefore, allow us the practice of becoming self-aware. Within self awareness practice, theories such as Yin and Yang become fundamental, as does TCM knowledge skill us with capabilities. Of which then can help us forge an ability for self diagnoses, and can also give us an ability for delivering treatments (Qigong), for our general health issues. At the most basic and deep level, TCM treatment seeks to balance Yin and Yang energy within each person. In this our Qigong development, we can become attuned to our energy and perform within our sensed need for harmony balance, as our life pathway seeks to fulfil it. Once the ancient theories of TCM learned through the 'Dragon Fire Qigong'; and produced through- Five Elemental Phases; Eight Tri Gram and Yin/Yang theories, here within expressed, are understood. Yin and Yangs importance will draw you closer to the universal energies of life in essence, governed through 'spirit light in self.'

You and Your Life how Yin and Yang apply

You may wonder how Yin and Yang through Qigong apply to you in life, in connection to any health issues, or that which may have brought you to Qigong. TCM theories have some meaning to your own lived experience, that's the point? First, the theory of Yin-Yang tells us that at the macrocosmic level, all things seek balance and rebalancing back into a state of harmony.

This could be ridiculed by the construct of negative life moments creating overwhelm, that with which we cannot adjust frequently enough to know, within ourselves a bigger picture ensures. Yes, there is ceaseless change, yet through these movements, a flow at its deepest level is creating hope toward harmony, your intentions to find yourself balanced is harmony establishing once again.

Yang and Yin being two expressions of energy embodying a Universal law, thus ensuring all things remain seeking harmony or balance. It's often difficult to sense harmony on a smaller scale, as within the world around us. Therefore, it isn't always apparent in this, a world of human dilemmas. With disharmonies created and producing turmoil, especially when placed into our busy yet somewhat complex modern lives. We are left thinking? To seminally understand Yin and Yang, harmony is the knowing that created forces have universal framework; these underlying factors, impacts within us and in essence! Harmony; is the ground with which upon we walk, talk and breathe a living soul attachment, in one way that is uniquely yours.

TCM's healing approach has this, a great partnership within Qigong is an assistance within your life, to take a look at how your life style or circumstance has lead to this moment, we may actually be creating our own health issues? Yet for most people this process happens over time (gaining wisdom). Others may see this approach building up, as it comes to them in moments of great insight (knowledge based learning).

From this a Qigong-TCM perspective, treating symptoms caused by emotions, patterns of thought, or the continual influence of societal belief systems. Those systems created through commercial lifestyle, then allowed to impart material based worldly system approaches, is out of balance? Therefore, it is just better to understand these issues, work from within to change these root causes and their problems? The entire fluctuation within this universal pattern, is one that is designed for the establishing and creation of your true balance and harmony.

Formed through this perspective, understanding enables a more peaceful view, one which opens up our sense of this world and our partnership within it. When people hear such sayings as, in a spiritual sense be likened to the expression "on Earth as in Heaven." It can reveal the sense again, of a: Universal law"- balancing of all things, is about creation and it's maintaining of harmony, wouldn't the limitless power of such an energy, if supporting your own efforts, help to create harmony in your own body and being? This is a truth only those whom seek to discover their partnership, within their life pathway, could deliver.

As is within this deep healing system (TCM- Qigong) the practitioner understands and applies Yin and Yang theory, helping to harmonise our bodies; heart, mind, Xin, and spirit, within our nature.

So now realising from this and other possible forms you've studied, such as here- (TCM). Yin and Yang are these interrelated forces placed together with the concept of Qi energy, connect within the foundation of Eastern medicine. Yin and Yang are mutually exclusive and together form a whole, from absolute existence in this realm, to that which, institutes two energies forged to become this universal entity and in balance, constitutes a state of harmony and health. When out of balance, it will indicate possible illness.

From this in a medical perspective, the relationship of Yin and Yang forms into this, a general basis, for all diagnoses and treatment protocols. In such a clinical example, would be a person whom has Liver Fire; with signs such as headaches, flushed face, and an incensed feeling of anger, exhibiting a disharmony, from a percentage of differing levels of Yin/Yang energy; 70% Yang and 30% Yin; reveals an excess of Yang energy.

To look then at how this may have become, look at your living environments as connections are made, one would search for the reasons, seeking information that supports, all that which is leading to this excessive Yang symptomatology.
    This information below discusses the Yin/Yang theory and

clinical applications in the process of using Qigong/Nei gong elementals, to relieve the symptoms and lead to our body-mind harmony, back to a level of re-harmonisation; so within the balance of Yin/Yang, and "Five Element Phase" theories, internal health can connect to a possible (Wellness diet or herbal medicine prescribed), performed within this book though; are the methods 'Meditations Harmony and Balance Stretching'.

As the principle balance of internal vital body energy is produced in the harmony of Yin organs (Zang- solid): Heart, Spleen, Lungs, Kidneys, and Liver. They are also in direct connection of energy flow through the system of harmonised connection.

The Yang organs (Fu-hollow), including the Small Intestines, Stomach, Large Intestines, Urinary Bladder, and Gall Bladder, adapt to the exchange that automatically occurs through the natural cycles of internal vital body energy balance. Yet, they follow a difference, as each organ has its own Qi energy vibrational element and source of functional relativity of internal harmonisation. Yin organs nourish the body with essence, while Yang organs flush or excrete through energy function. Therefore, the response lies in the connection to how they interact and naturally progress to the benefit of both the Yin/Yang couples and the fluctuations in balance, within the (Theory of Five-Element structure).

Yin and Yang Theory Qigong

Through the essence of the "Dao De Jing" by Laozi, "Dao" is defined as: So! An ancient philosophy that gives us (The one universe gave birth to two energies- light and firmament). These two aspects became known as Yin and Yang - this polarity of difference that presents the "Great principle of Yang and Yin." Resides within this premise, a polarity formed into this structural existing universe, that from of which we know, and foundation of all our known creation, this basis of Qi forms within all things and movement or change, thus the field in which energy and matter engage; such as formation and interaction, cessation, and transmutation.

Yin, originally an ideogram as in- "shady side of a tree," came to refer to the negative or dark aspects, passivity, coolness, moon and water, softness/yielding- (martial terms), internal aspects, and lower dimensions of a field, form, or energy system. It also incorporates the highest density of matter, firmament from earth.

Yang, originally meaning "sunny side of a tree," denotes positive energy, light, external aspects, activity, such as the sun and fire, warmth, strength- (martial terms). It represents the lightest forms of energy and from the highest presence, rising heat or from above "Heaven or Celestial- solar."

As we are now aware? It is crucial to understand that Yin and Yang are not two distinctly different types of energy, but rather two complementary yet opposite poles in any form (earth), function (movement-change), or energy field (universe). Furthermore, as the original ideograms indicate, Yin and Yang are mutually transmutable - as the planet turns and the angle of the sun changes, the sunny side becomes shady and vice versa; the Yin side lights up and becomes Yang.

Through Qigong we become aware of Yin and Yangs polarity, and as this manifestation aspect does include human body energy systems. For instance, our breathe, inhalation Yin-Yang and exhalation Yang-Yin. In the body; upper, outer, and back sections are termed Yang in perspective; as lower, inner, inside and front parts are Yin.

As our Yin belongs to Blood! Yang would become energy- Spirit fire. Our head represents above or celestial a Yang- as our sacrum the base of our Celestial function 'Brain and spine', is therefore the Yin connect. The internal organs follow a Yin solid- Nourish in (Zang); whilst hollow (Fu) organs are the cleanse-out release; Yang. In mind our thoughts could be construed as Yang, and feelings Yin; these polarities are revealed again and again throughout the Chi Boxing/Qigong context. Within all of our human body form, (body, essence, and mind). The most common and important pairs of functional facets representing Yin/Yang are these:

- **Prenatal and Postnatal:** All levels of human life being prenatal or postnatal. The prenatal is the primordial potential (Yuan Qi) we bring into our lives at birth, the sexual glands of males and females, pass this on through procreation and in the conception of another being. Postnatal is produced throughout our life with the advent from taking in of food, water, and air, thus forging within our blood, lymph, hormones, along with other vital fluids of our bodies.

- **Fire and Water:** This symbolisation of Fire as an archetypal energy, representing Yang, and Water symbolising Yin. In the human body energy system, Fire being a temporal form of energy and fuelled by metabolism, respiration. Water is more the primordial energy ancient and from past (ancestral), stored in the glands. Ordinarily over the course of our life, this Fire energy tends to flare upward and dissipate itself (affecting Heart/mind), or sometimes this creates disturbance of thought harmony, conflicting emotions, also formed from excessive or strenuous exercise. Water energy from the glands-nodes, brain, kidneys follows the downward path out, sometimes dissipating through sexual activity, also stress.

Meditations Harmony and Balanced Stretching

The internal alchemy (Nei Dan) as a purposeful connection within Daoist practice known as Nei-gong (internal work) is to help reverse the untrained course of deliveries 'Fire and Water' energies contain. Add an awareness into our being, a way to prolong our life essence. This is done by maintaining control over the influence of Fire energies that can form in the head, heart, and solar plexus. Instead through our awareness and knowledge of the major channels, this refining and recirculating of it, or the storing down into the lower wellness centre "Xia" below the belly button. Will then at the same time allow us to promote the precious Water energy, ordinarily dissipated through sexual activity or stress. To then conserve and raise upward through the sacral forging, Gu Sui-marrow and spinal channels into the head, where it nourishes the faculties of the Mind/Spirit.

- **Movement and Stillness:** Yang activity manifests movement; Yin contains calm, cooling and quietude, creating stillness. As previously stated; when activity is prolific, this physical activity causes Fire to flare upwards burning up our bodies energy reserves of essence, whereas meditation, stillness, calms the mind body system, cooling the fire within, helping conserve vital resources. Thus, tranquil practicing methods helps preserve, giving health benefits and longevity. In Qigong, the practice of "movement and stillness" brings balance; internal stillness of the Mind is balanced with external movements of the body in exercise, thus the presence of internal energy through stillness in sitting meditation forms settle the Spirit/Self.

- **Internal (Nei) and External (Wai):** External aspects of Qigong practice, known as Wai-gong, include all body movements and belong to Yang, while internal work, called Nei-gong, primarily involves the Mind and Breath and the deeper introspection of within, therefore belongs to Yin.

As summarised: In concept Yang and Yin theory, is a generalisation of two polar complements, such as positive, negative, or hard and soft; related to these complementary opposites can be the use of labels in-which to describe two opposite things or two opposite aspects contained within one thing.

Dragon Fire Qigong

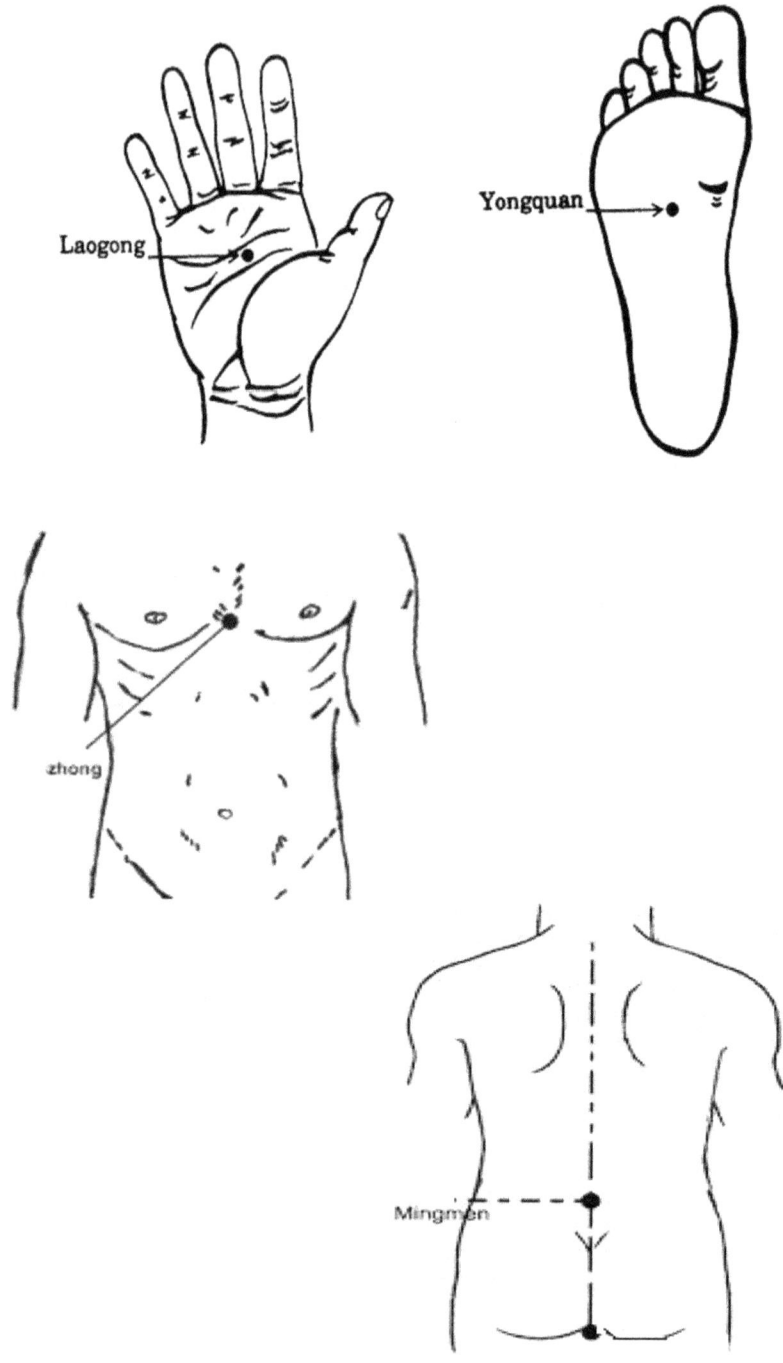

Meditations Harmony and Balanced Stretching

Dragon Fire Qigong

Meditations Harmony and Balanced Stretching

SECTION III:

SEATED SEED CONCEPTION FORM/8 TRI GRAMS

+ CENTRE

SEATED SEED CONCEPTION FORM/8 TRI GRAMS + CENTRE

Chapter 1 :

Because this construct or design of performance (eight tri grams) is derived from 'Ancient Chinese Philosophy' I still use the designed principled in my 'Dragon Fire Qigong' approach. But due to the fact that I do not utilise such things as divination purpose, (book of Yi Jing) or for that matter the construct of only Martial connect. My system is to display the very core of development into our physical body Pre-heaven {mother host and seed within growing}, first of all something had to be created- The Heavens! Then from this within creation, formed the life energy-us? To then lead onto our performing; once grown into life (Soul-Breath) we become tied to the energy of performing as living self (Post- Heaven). This construct leads onto the awareness of:

Five elements now connect to and within the construct of our producing structural intent to perform energy movements, of which enable us to promote transmutation and energy designed for wellness, healing, and restorative purposes. How to incorporate this system in a balance and check formulation Mind/body constructs and reach uniformity of purpose.

Therefore, the system set out in Dragon Fire; is to understand the formation of our body structure and then this knowing construct can deliver energy through our self 'Qigong- Nei gong' formulations.

Meditations Harmony and Balanced Stretching

Seated: Seed Conception - Eight Trigrams and Centre

Preparation: This style of Qigong/Nei gong is practiced in a seated position, either on a chair (with a straight back, seated on the near edge) or cross-legged on a cushion or mat. Palms are placed facing down on the knees. Close your eyes, tuck in your chin, and hold your head as if an intention of thought is drawing you up through the Baihui point to further straighten your spine, allowing energy to flow smoothly through the body's circuit. Place the tip of your tongue on the palate just behind the teeth, keeping it relaxed. Breathe naturally through your nose, in a relaxed state, letting your mind become calm. Meditate on the three energy centres for a few minutes, beginning with the Huiyin, then Baihui, and concentrating on the Xia-wellness centre. As you inhale, allow Qi to rise up the back along the 'Du Mai,' starting from the base of your spine (sacrum), following the points of your energy channel to the Baihui point, then over the head to Shang and under to an upper lip point just below the nose.

Focus on your exhale, moving from a point in the middle of your lower lip, down the front of your body 'Ren Mai,' to Xia, and then onward to Huiyin, completing a cycle of this inner energy. This breathing pattern, called circulation breath, is performed three times between each section of the seated Seed Conception form, initially to the left and then repeated to the right on the second phase.

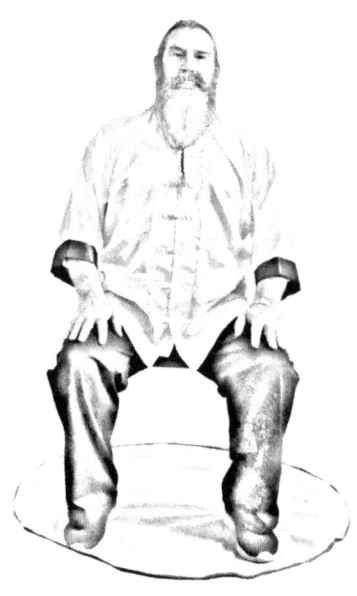

Dragon Fire Qigong

Begin first through: Initiate Spirit; the sparkling eyes, then perform the sacral pump of Dragon Fire.

Open eyes to look with sparkle; with a sense of; from your inner smile, move your eyes to see. Firstly, look up, then down; moving only your eyes for a count of twelve times (up and down count as one). Then look with sparkle; horizontally-left to right 12 times. Then in a diagonal; starting from left top-down to right. Then right top, down to left 12 times each side. Then circle your eyes; firstly, from left to right 9 times, then reverse right to left 9 times, before pausing with eyes clamped shut, then opening, to shut and open 9 times.

Sitting on the chair edge or near front of chair or if on a cushion? 'Warm the sacrum with dragon spirals', nine circles pressing through the sitting bones and with hands focused into the Kua, as if holding a Qi ball, right to left in a figure 8 movement. Then bring this warmed energy through your hands up the front spine, to the head; connect palm energy onto Shang (upper wellness centre)- middle forehead, with palms then moving out to temples, then draw the Qi downwards from face to chest, down onto knees. Rest.

Breathe; then take two circulation Breaths.

Meditations Harmony and Balanced Stretching

The Waterfall from the Mountain - baths within.

This exercise stimulates both Du Mai and Ren Mai and warms Ming Men and the spine, opens and closes the cranial and sacral pumps interacting with the uniformity of macrocosmic actions and brings the para- sympathetic nervous system into play. Thusly; making the 'Gu Sui-marrow' more enriched and fluid; or as a saying, the spine becomes more juicy with 'Jing Qi' energy (Marrow).

Breathe in; then on the out-breath focus the intention to expel the breath as you arch your back inwards with your head moving forwards towards your knees. Then, as you begin your in-breath - rise with your back arching upwards and the reverse, to bring your trunk back to your starting position like a rolling flow. Do this movement as if you are bathing in a Waterfall to cleanse your; Head, Back, Face, and Chest.

Repeat Six times: with a calming breath pause in-between the movements, before completing the sequence again. Breathing too deeply may increase the dizziness sensation- too much oxygenation into the blood, so remember to pause between the movements.

Breathe; then take two circulation Breaths.

Dragon Fire Qigong

1. **Above**: Present from the essence of heart and soul, the strength to press up (hands held palm up, in front of your Zhong region). Press up above the Shang slightly, then turn hands inward to press inside shoulder width with elbows bent, feeling the energy within. Return palms to Zhong holding energy before turning hands over, left under right.

2. **Earthed**: Concentrate the energy ball compressed between Abdomen and lower Abdomen-Yin/Yang symbol; forming from the base hand, left palm up from the bottom on the side one focuses on in the aspect of delivery—left represents forming of the universe and within.

3. **Water**: Swap the poles of the two palms, turning in opposite directions to churn the Waters of energy within; Yin/Yang, double spiral movement for stomach, spleen, Kidneys, rising up to the abdomen.

4. **Fire**: The top hand scoops down to Xia to catch the Fire energy within, raising joyful wellness energy from deep within, palms holding an energy ball resembling, supporting the heavens- the Moon; this is dependent on the directional focus, with hands held up above the Shang line with one palm scooping energy up and the other near the Shang point, turn from the centre to outside left on the out-breath hold; then breathe when coming back to centre, the inner core and the Heart.

5. **Central axis**: Yin and Yang: From the extended Fire hand position, alternate the palm toward the core, down and around to form the bottom press of the Yin/Yang. Stretch (left hand from high to inside upper left thigh), while the other hand circles back up through the Zhong region, stretching up from the central core-throat/mouth region. Both palms face the direction in a pressing motion toward the centre of the movement pattern. Lunar=left. Solar=right. Yin and Yang. Hold position to form strength in the core.

6. **Mountain**: From the previous Yin hand position, raise that arm up and across to the opposite arm to form the energy flow pressing out into the formation of a mountain. Both palms press outward level with the abdomen (solar plexus), creating central contraction, strengthening Kidneys and Meridians of the waist, and stretching Yin meridians of Arms. Hold position to form strength in the core.

7. **Smoke**: From the central position, move the hand on the mountain side (left). Vertically rise up behind the other hand slightly under elbow-palm facing down, spiralling

Meditations Harmony and Balanced Stretching

stretch of arm meridians Yin and Yang. Hold position to form strength in the core.

8. **Volcano**: Draw the leading hand down and press into Xia, palm facing down, while the other palm rises up to Shang. Hold the pose as you stretch looking left side, contraction fills Qi in the three Wellness centres.

9. **Wind and Clouds**: Bring the elbow of your raised arm down to the level of the abdomen as you pivot front centre once more. The hand scoops out, down, and around and back again, as the other hand does the same - spin gets Qi to stimulate the blood. Converge hands into the central core, then bathe the Baihui before ending in Kua. Draw energy around the belt channel to bathe Ming men with Hegu points - nine times, then press Qi massage along your hips, buttocks, and outer thighs, over knees, and up inner thighs. Rest palms in your lap once more 'Calm Serene'.

Start with palms facing up in your lap, Xia:Pre-Heaven

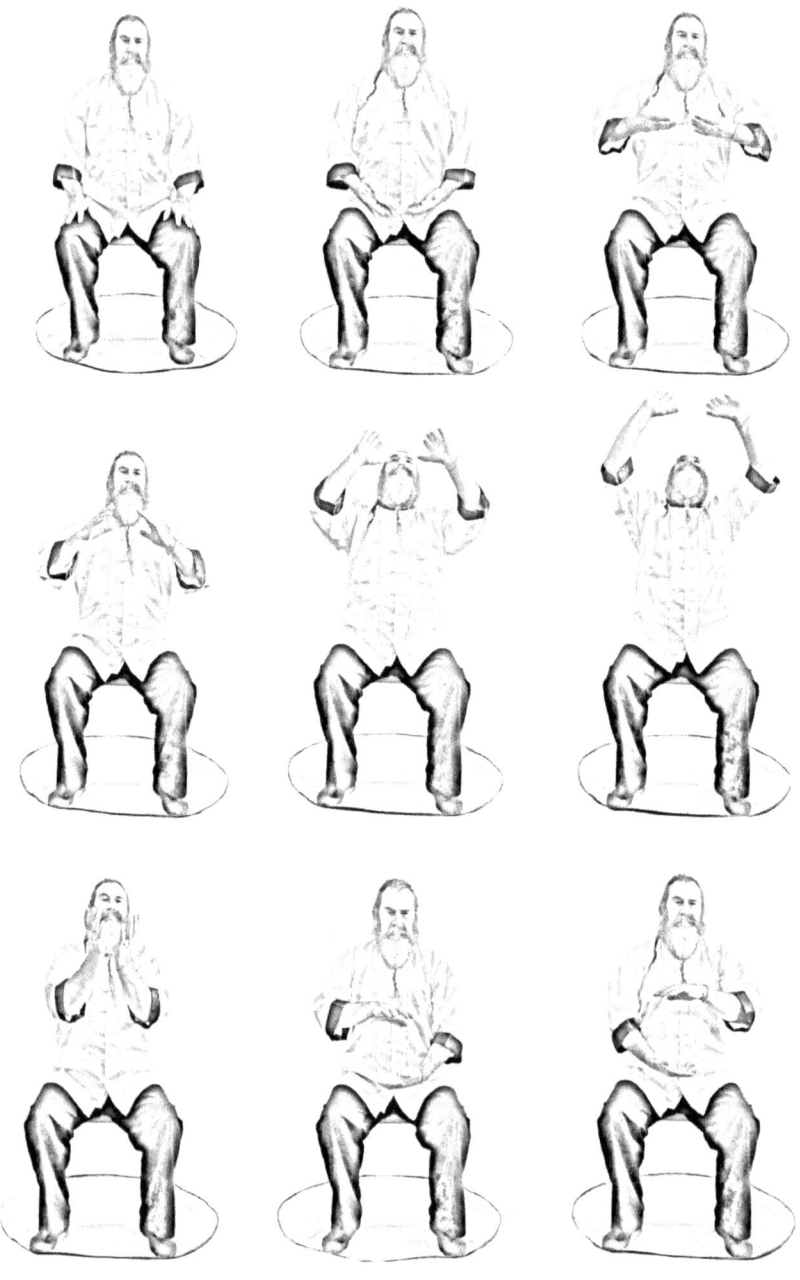

8 Tri Grams + Centre- press Heaven and Earth 1-2

Meditations Harmony and Balanced Stretching

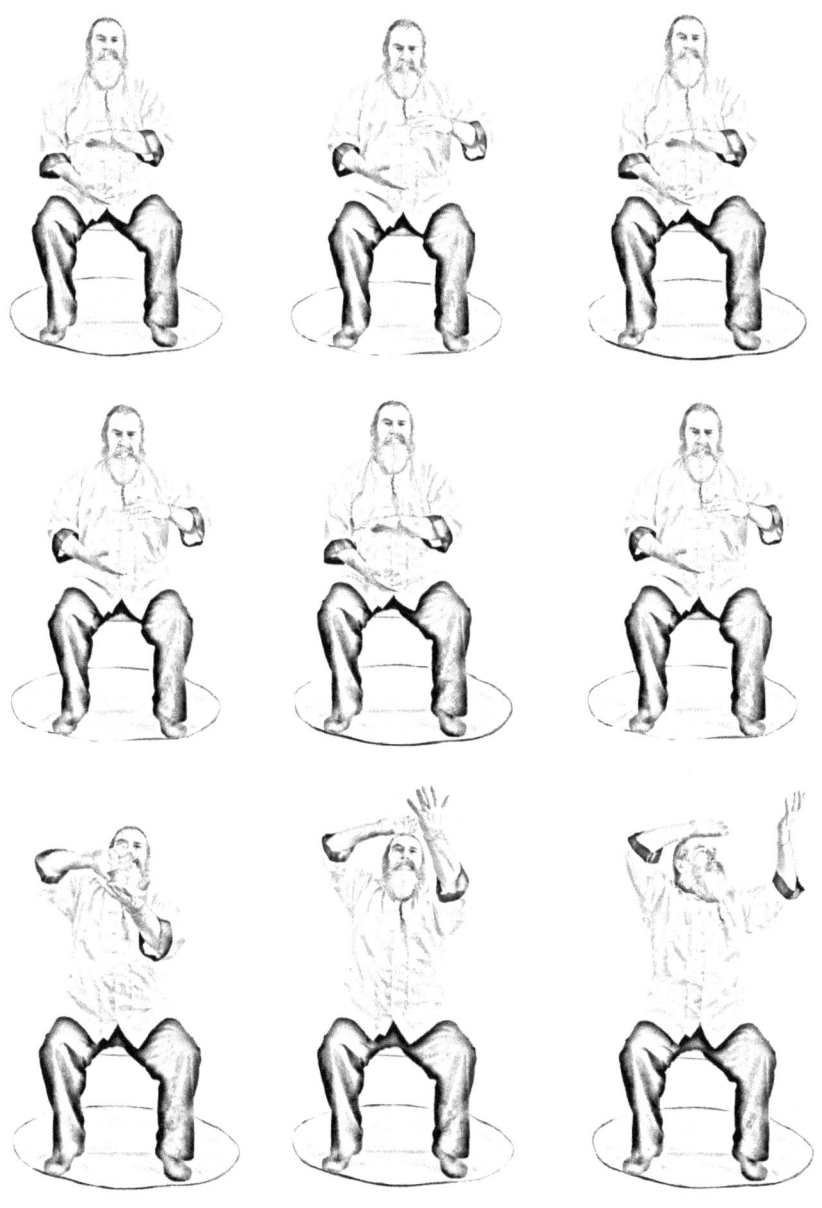

8 Tri Grams + Centre- Water - Fire 3-4

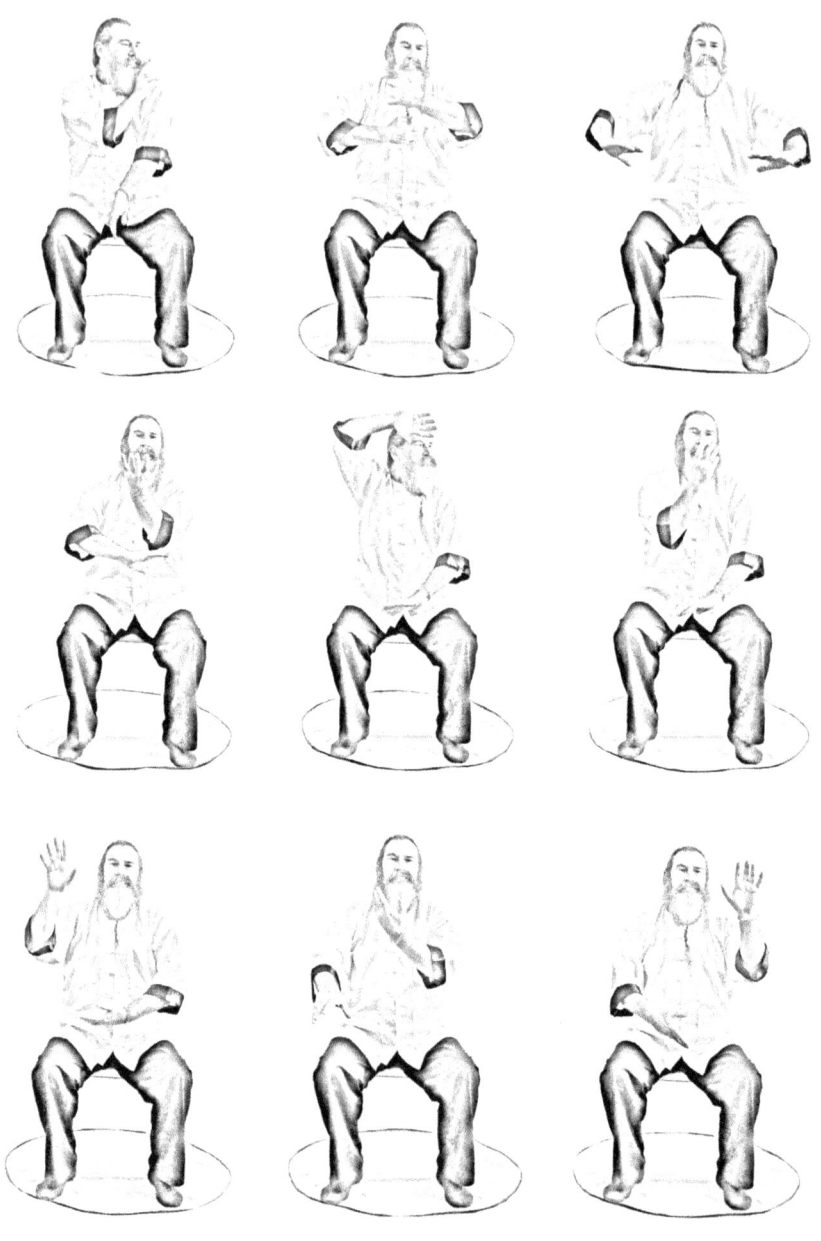

8 Tri Grams + Centre- Central Axis- Mountain- Smoke- Volcano- Cloud/Wind 5-6-7-8-9

Meditations Harmony and Balanced Stretching

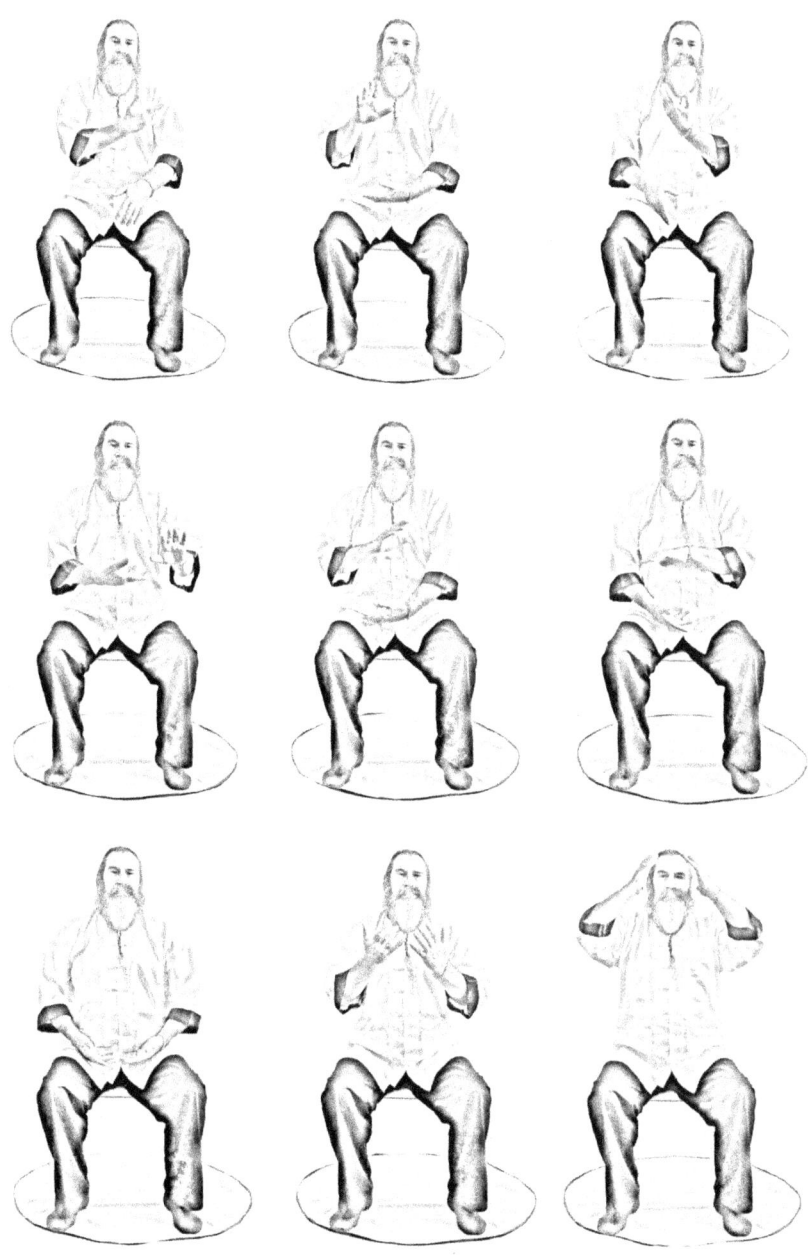

8 Tri Grams + Centre- Cloud/Wind 9

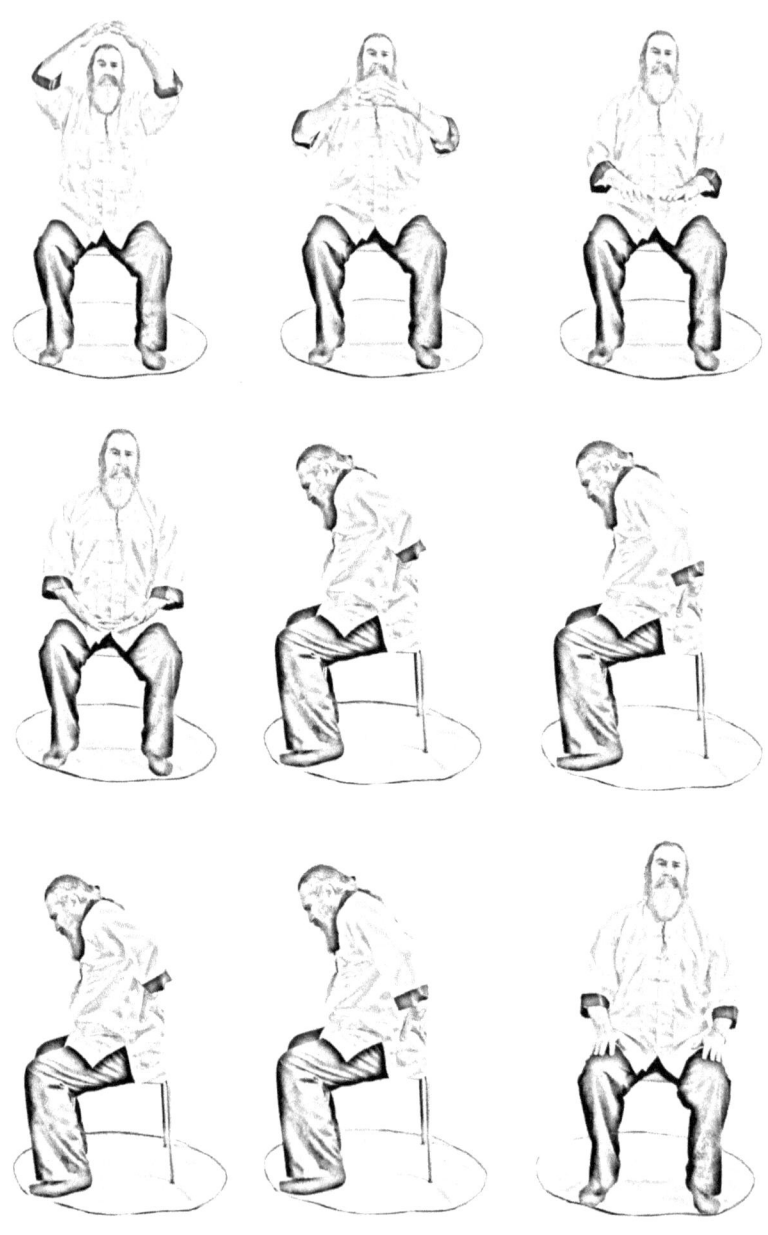

8 Tri Grams + Centre- Settle- bath Ming Men 9a

Meditations Harmony and Balanced Stretching

Then the breathing pattern, called circulation breath, is performed again three times but as the energy breath of the "Chong Mai "of the seated Seed Conception form, then repeat formation of movements to the right. As the right side represents formed into readiness of being born and the life entirety.

10. Repeated on the right side direction after three Chong Mai breaths. Represents sealing the qualities of Post-heaven life formed. 5 becomes Wood life energy as Yin and Yang, 7 becomes the lake, were life is grown from; 8 becomes Thunder- soul breath voice.

Start with palms facing up in your lap, Xia:Post-Heaven

1. **Above**: Present from the essence of heart and soul, the strength to press up (hands held palm up, in front of your Zhong region). Press up above the Shang slightly, then turn hands inward to press inside shoulder width with elbows bent, feeling the energy within. Return palms to Zhong holding energy before turning hands over, right under left.

2. **Earthed**: Concentrate the energy ball compressed between Abdomen and lower Abdomen-Yin/Yang symbol; forming from the base hand, right palm up from the bottom on the side one focuses on in the aspect of delivery—right represents earth has formed life essence.

3. **Water**: Swap the poles of the two palms, turning in opposite directions to churn the Waters of energy within; Yin/Yang, double spiral movement for stomach, spleen, Kidneys, rising up to the abdomen.

4. **Fire**: The top hand scoops down to Xia to catch the Fire energy within, raising joyful wellness energy from deep within, palms holding an energy ball resembling the supporting heaven- the Sun; this is dependent on the directional focus, hands held up above the Shang line with one palm scooping energy up and the other near the Shang point, turning from the centre to outside on the out-breath hold; then breathe when coming back to centre, strengthening the inner core and the Heart.

5. **Central axis**: Yin and Yang: From the extended Fire hand position, alternate the palm toward the core, down and around to form the bottom press of the Yin/Yang. Stretch (right hand from high to inside upper right thigh), while the other hand circles back up through the Zhong region, stretching up from the central core-throat/mouth region. Both palms face the direction in a pressing motion toward

the centre of the movement pattern. Lunar=left. Solar=right. Yin and Yang. Hold position to form strength in the core.

6. **Mountain**: From the previous Yin hand position, raise that arm up and across to the opposite arm to form the energy flow pressing out into the formation of a mountain. Both palms press outward level with the abdomen (solar plexus), creating central contraction, strengthening Kidneys and Meridians of the waist, and stretching Yin meridians of Arms. Hold position to form strength in the core.

7. **Lake**: From the central position, move the hand on the mountain side (right). Vertically rise up behind the other hand slightly under elbow-palm facing down, spiralling stretch of arm meridians Yin and Yang. Hold position to form strength in the core.

8. **Thunder**: Draw the leading hand down and press into Xia, palm facing down, while the other palm rises up to Shang. Hold the pose as you stretch looking right side, contraction fills Qi in the three Wellness centres.

9. **Wind and Clouds**: Bring the elbow of your raised arm down to the level of the abdomen as you pivot front centre once more. The hand scoops out, down, and around and back again, as the other hand does the same - spin gets Qi to stimulate the blood. Converge hands into the central core, then bathe the Baihui before ending in Kua. Draw energy around the belt channel to bathe Ming men with Hegu points - nine times, then press Qi massage along your hips, buttocks, and outer thighs, over knees, and up inner thighs. Rest palms in your lap once more 'Calm Serene'.

This form 1/ Eight Tri Grams Seed; connects to the three other Eight Tri gram forms in Dragon Fire Qigong/Nei gong:

2/Umbilical-Embryonic

3/Standing Eight Trigrams + Centre

4/Lunar-Solar Circle Walking Eight Trigrams + Centre.

Meditations Harmony and Balanced Stretching

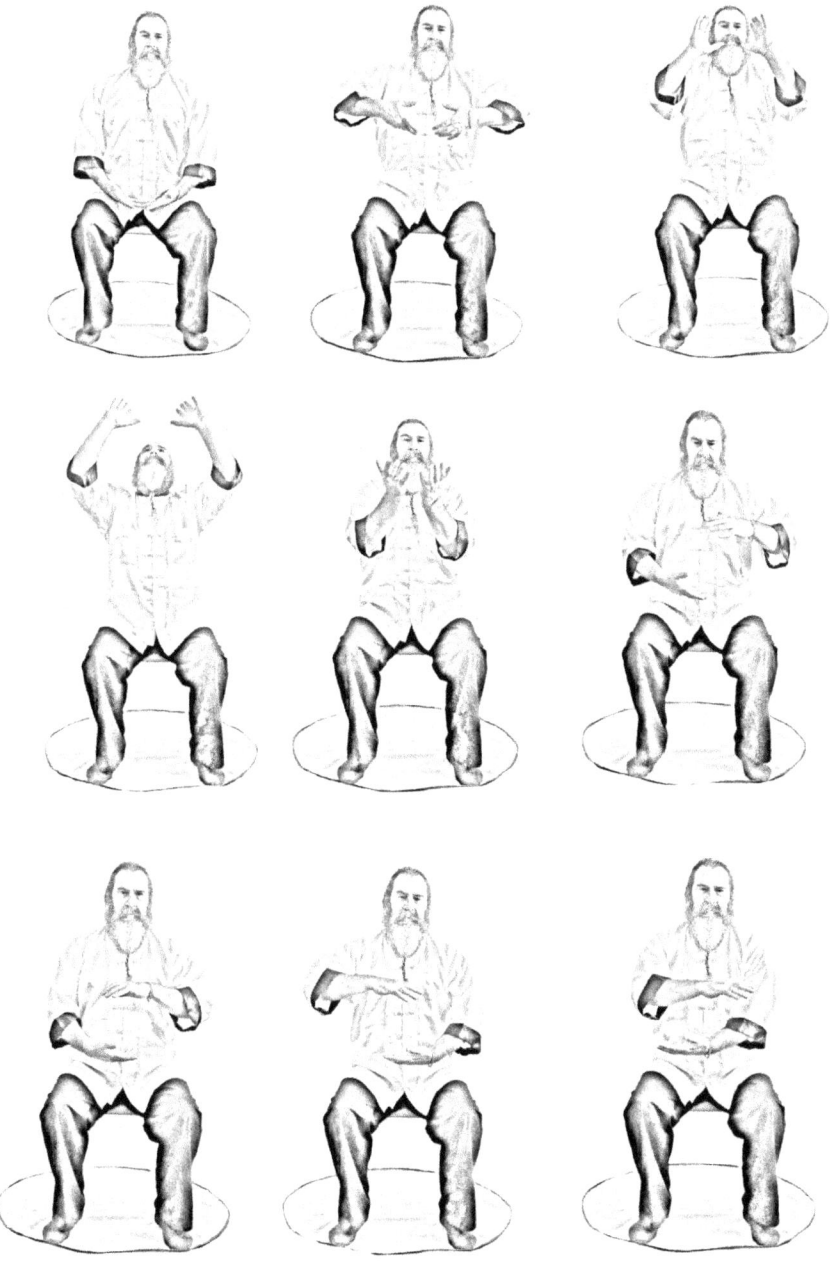

8 Tri Grams + Centre- Post-Heaven and Earth 1-2

Dragon Fire Qigong

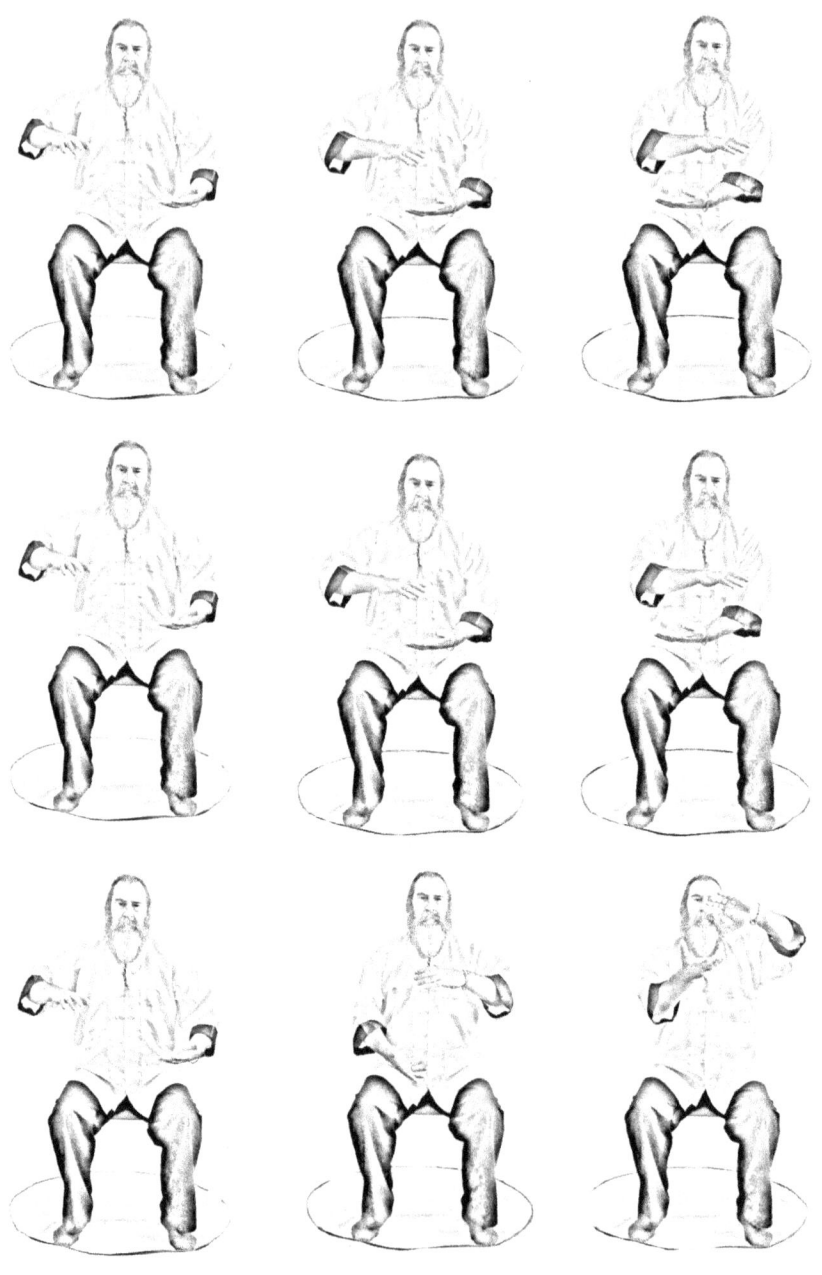

**8 Tri Grams + Centre- Central Axis- Fire- Mountain-
Lake- Thunder 4-5-6-7-8**

Meditations Harmony and Balanced Stretching

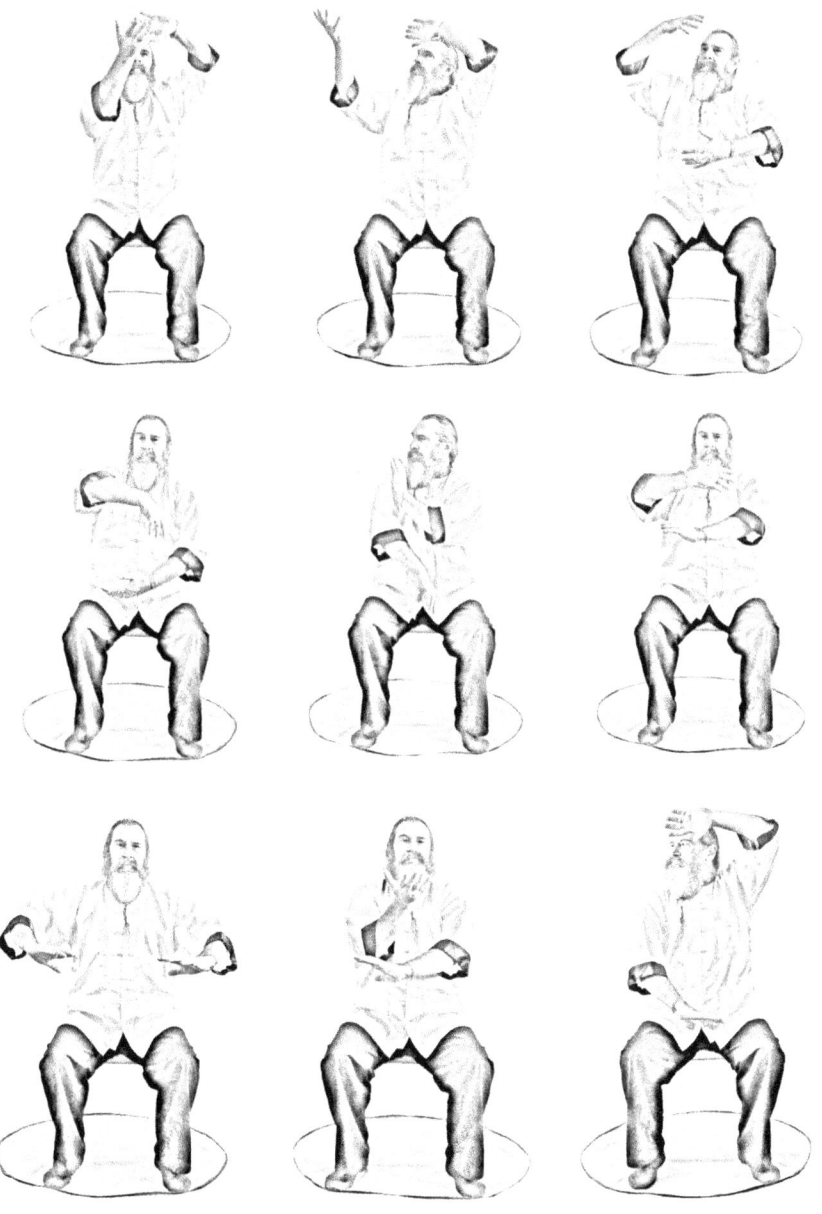

8 Tri Grams + Centre- Central Axis- Fire- Mountain- Lake- Thunder 4-5-6-7-8

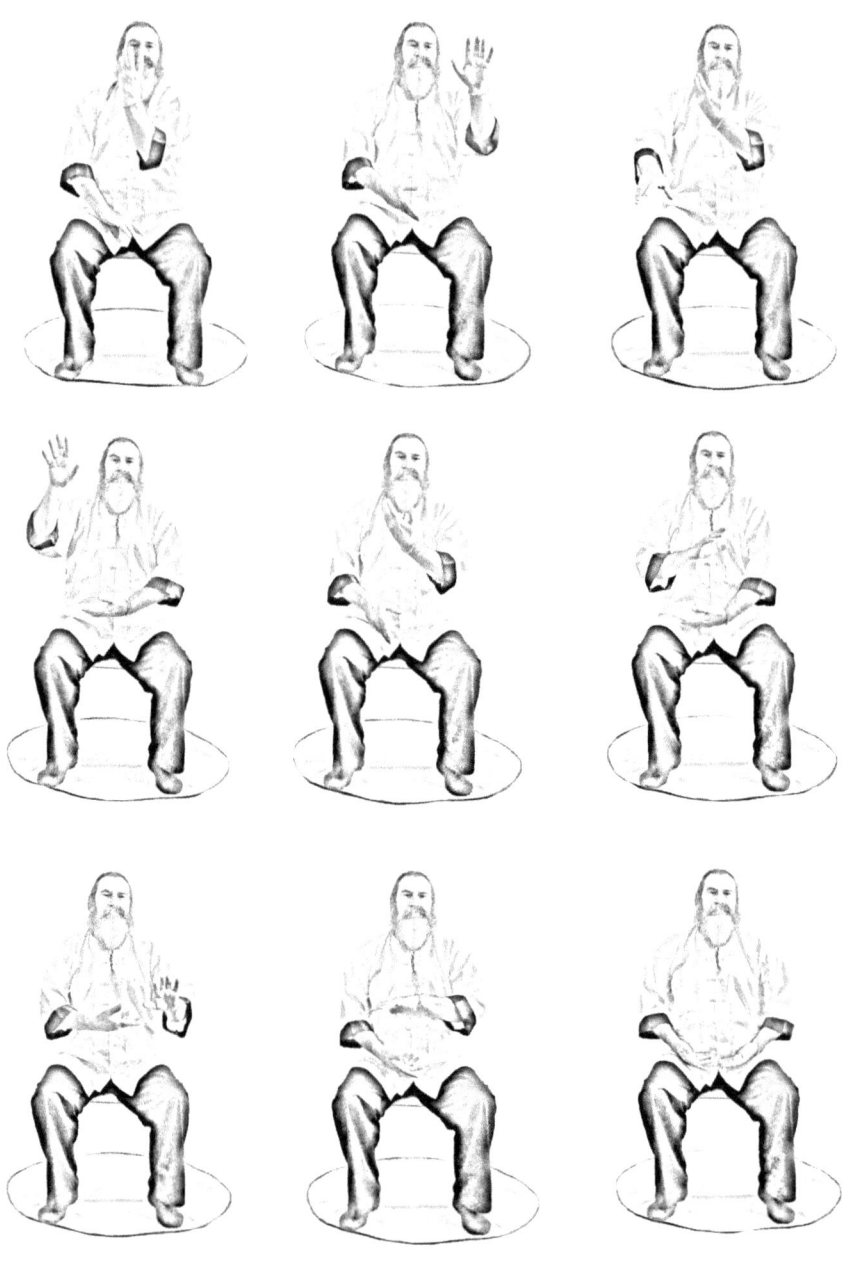

8 Tri Grams + Centre- Cloud/Wind 9

Meditations Harmony and Balanced Stretching

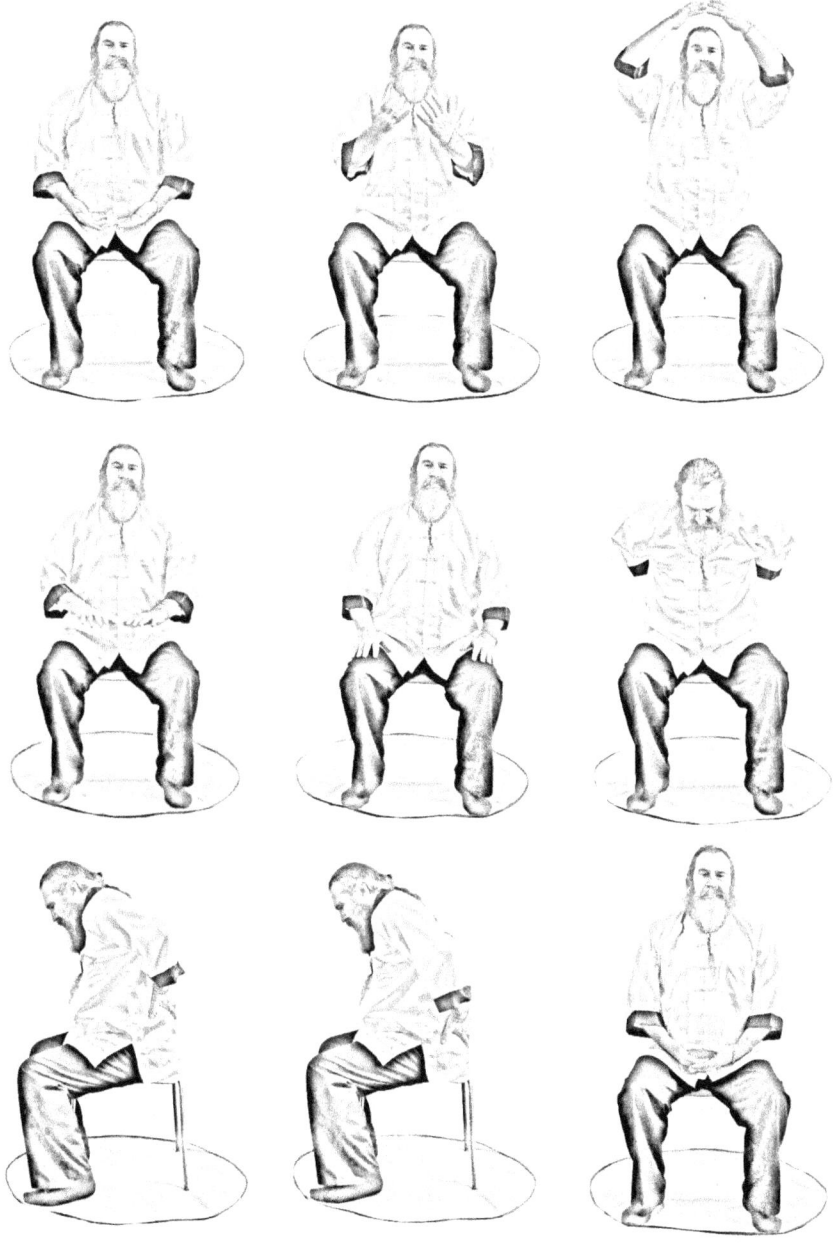

**8 Tri Grams + Centre- Settle- bath Ming Men
9a Settle in Xia Serene calm**

Chapter 2:

-what does this include

Bāguà to Feng Shui belief, the positive Qi energy in one's life, environment, and living area should be balanced. Off-balanced areas or aspects of life can be readjusted with corresponding items and symbols in corresponding colours, leading to a harmonious and balanced Qi energy flow. The Qi energy is supposed to improve life, while one is living in harmony with nature. In Feng Shui, the Bāguà template or map is used to stabilise, protect, adjust, or restore balance in one's life by analysing or structuring any given space.

In "Dragon Fire" and "Chi Boxing; Qigong," I have reformulated the theology and ideology of this form to incorporate a new essence of intrinsic discovery based on the concept of having a Bāguà and the Eight Trigrams. With the content changed to suit the "Pre-Heaven Bāguà" to represent energies whilst Heaven forming and Earth as Pre-Life, and the later Bāguà—Post-Earth and Heaven—to represent earthly formations based on the 'living matter' energy, or in this case, the 'Wood Element' of carbon-based life forms, in the generation of Spirit/Self and Soul/Breath.

Therefore, each section of the structured spaces in the Bāguà will now encompass through 'Chi Boxing; Dragon Fire Qigong' the 'Elements' forming the firmaments of Being (existence from) and will incorporate a new issuance of subject matter. For those who have delved deeply into the Philosophy and Theology, such as the Yi Jing (I Ching) and the process of their divinations, which entail this formulated context, its believed to relate to various aspects of life, divided into categories concerning physical and emotional aspects, like family, career, futures, outcomes, and pathways ventured, etc.

There has in my case; merely been a slight change to my represented formula Within Pre-Heaven; in that the "Dui" (lake marsh) is to be replaced with "Smoke" connects through the Volcano as part of the five elements (the centre being Yin/Yang, which becomes the Wood element in life's post-heaven), thus the beginning firmament exists, and then in the post "Earth and Heaven Bāguà," it turns into the essence of marsh/lake connects to thunder (soul breath voiced), thereby becoming connected to "Absolute Existence" within the realm of living matter. Therefore, combining two important structures of Yi (Will) in both Spirit formed (belonging to Eternal Light of Absolute Existence!) and Soul Breath (Eternal Spirit Light Immortal) life-body formed; in connection with the 'Eight Trigrams' and the 'Five Element' theory through the Yin and Yang completions.

Both types of Bāguà have been developed long before in the Book of Changes—Yi Jing (I Ching), which describes the cosmology and philosophy of Ancient China. The basic ideas are balance-through opposites and acceptance of change. The basis of my Chi Boxing; Qigong and therefore also my Dragon Fire Qigong system does not entail their Ancient Chinese formulations to the extent of becoming only their related opinion. As I have formulated this reasoning upon what I, as an individual person, can aspire to become in reflection of my own understanding of self. This does not include their dogma and reticulated scenarios of the supposition; their past is for myself only. As I have developed my own understanding through Dao into the perspectives of my being. Cosmology in my 'Dragon Fire' is of the Spirit/Self, not the personifications of planets and stars, etc.

Both my Bāguà are associated with the eight compass directions; both Bāguà use the cardinal directions. These cardinal directions are determined by the marker-points within the Self, not as the Ancients did with celestial phenomena—stars of the 'northern hemisphere' of which I have rarely seen! But this Theory can and has been transplanted into myself; in the arrival of persona becoming Spirit/Self as "Tiger, Dragon, Eagle" forged into the directions through Eight Trigrams and the Five Element structure of Physical Self.

This is altered into the representation of the Theology of "Dragon Fire" and the "Chi Boxing" elementals. Will be stated as in the first phase of performing 'Eight Tri Gram' movement form- to the left side of the person. Is then performed as, the energy forming of: from heaven- earth forms. So in this case it represents that the organ blood system represented in forming is Pre- birth the (foetus) inside the person; or Nourish- in, Spleen- Stomach blood connect system and the forming of the structure of our body building first stage. As does the heavens form through chaos into structured harmony firstly, before settling into being calm enough for living matter to form. Thus the first phase including Volcano and Smoke-lake, is the forming before settling into readiness for birth- or.

The second phase or delivery on the right side of the person represents the system of blood through the Liver system connect. Is now the spirit is ready to be born or for that matter that life has formed the calm- Water Lake of life forming and the Thunder of Voice soul breath. In this book we will only focus on the first Bāguà formed Fu Xi from the Ho Tu, as the second Bāguà from the Lo Shu represents the using in Five Element presentation.

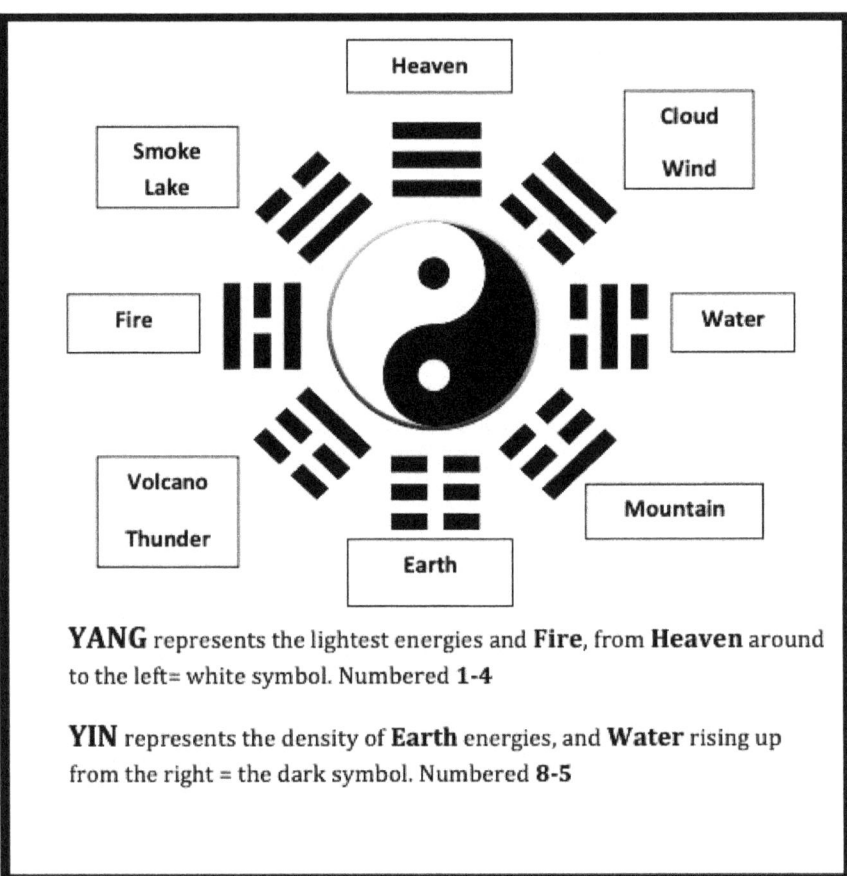

YANG represents the lightest energies and **Fire**, from **Heaven** around to the left = white symbol. Numbered **1-4**

YIN represents the density of **Earth** energies, and **Water** rising up from the right = the dark symbol. Numbered **8-5**

Meditations Harmony and Balanced Stretching

Dragon Fire Qigong

SECTION IV:
LONGEVITY FORMS

Longevity Forms of Dragon Fire

In Dragon Fire Qigong; I have designed the forms of Longevity, to correspond with the Soul Breath

1st, open breath sequence; this then leads into the intrinsic formulation of body Qi transformation, introduced through the umbilical press area, and circulation of the Dai Mai - Belt Channel.

2nd. Represents both internal accumulation rises from Xia and also to represent the spirit of the self, formulates energy within the lower wellness centre, to then be drawn upwards in an ascending manner, connecting lower body energy, to our mind and brain- Tai Yang (temples) and Shang (front of forehead). Therefore, from Xia lower wellness centre, upwards towards the head. To then once again settle or descend back through the central core front of spine- body, into lower wellness centre Xia.

3rd Longevity circuit, is to initiate these energies into our upper organ system; Heart and lungs. Instigated to introduce the Earthly body organs; Stomach, Large Intestine, Small Intestine, Kidney; Spleen/Pancreas-Liver; ascend to fill the 'Heaven' body organs Heart-Lungs, after connecting through the body flow from Xia. Into our Mind- Brain region, connecting Laogong points in an Qi flow up to and around the Tai Yang (temples). This flow then releases heat outwards from the side of head, to release in a press out in front of the Shang; extended. Energy is then drawn back towards the Yin Tang point between the eyebrows, to connect positive energy from the universe, to then press downwards into the body Xia.

4th stage is to take this repeating energy flow and step it out diagonally; first to the left side. With left foot stepping out left, and right foot pivots from ball and toes; by moving heel back. Forming the centre circle of gathering energy as you do so. As you are in left forward stance facing left diagonal, your feet are pressed in readiness to create the flow of Qi and Blood energy, in synchronicity of the hands and arms moving. This flow of Intrinsic Qi formulating around and through the body, enables the press of Qi Blood energy.

Designed to deliver smooth flowing and warming energy from bottom of the feet, up through the channels inside of legs. Then as you gather the intrinsic Qi energy of the lower Earth organs and Xia. Initiated from the pose of when standing after moving into diagonal, the palms facing up as if holding your intrinsic Qi formulations just gathered, are now delivering upwards to the Mind-brain, to once again press release, Tai Yang, then draw back into the Yin Tang. As you then descend through the press of Qi energy down to the inside middle left thigh. Connecting once more to the Blood energy from the legs. The flow of energy pressed through the legs, moves back and forth within the press and flow of arm, body, leg movements of Qi. This is then repeated to the right side, after a centring of energy flow to stabilise, then with an on flow affect, performed again diagonally through the arms and legs.

Meditations Harmony and Balanced Stretching

5th Stage is performed once the completion of both diagonal directions are complete, and you then centre your energy front facing. From this central position expand your stance from Mountain Stance High, into Mountain Stance Middle. This is done by moving toe out left first, in synchronicity of left hand arm performing cloud hands flow, as your left foot toes out- with your left hand moving centred left. Your right foot toes out with right hand in synchronicity of hand foot movements. Then as your hands form the circling once again; in cloud hands you then place left heel out, to create the balanced stance, as is also performed onto the right side. Completing the forming of a deeper stance- (Mountain Stance Yang), a wider platform of movement, and a readiness to press your Qi energy once again, into the next stage of energy transfer.

6th Stage is the forming an energy press from the stabilising of the Self in Mountain Stance, circulates the energy around the mountain with a Mountain press into then; support the Smoke-lake left, leads to Volcano and then Cloud-Wind. Representing the formulations of self change- (spleen system). This stage is to also represent the body forming structural changes, now in line with the 'Eight Tri Grams' of Dragon Fire. This then is performed onto the right side, (liver system) representing the structural formulations of change required in the body self, has performed the life energy it needs can lead on to Longevity. This right side formula is: Mountain press forms into then; supporting the 'Lake-Marsh'-water, leads to Thunder (soul breath) and then into Cloud-Wind.

This formulation of energy- Qi, Blood-Xue; body press is what allows the intrinsic Qi Formulations, to be a sense of 'Transmutation' and or transforming (Body-Mind-Breath) into a better performing structure, leading into a healthier 'Wellness' balance. Therefore, the body self, can hope to attain a longer life. In a deeper sense; this formulation and technique of Dragon fire, can also lead back to the Spirit self- in so much as your 'Spirit' becomes intwined with the sense of; look after your life and your soul breath.

As a platform performance, in collaboration with the Ba Duan Jin (seated method essence). This energy (Longevity) allows the complete standing body formed, in a structure that can easily, then be applied to this seated energy platform, allowed to create a physical readiness, for better performing seated and or meditative training.

Dragon Fire Qigong

1st, open breath sequence; press down then draw back up and press once more down. Connecting to Umbilical region and to spread Qi energy through the Dai Mai Belt Channel.

Meditations Harmony and Balanced Stretching

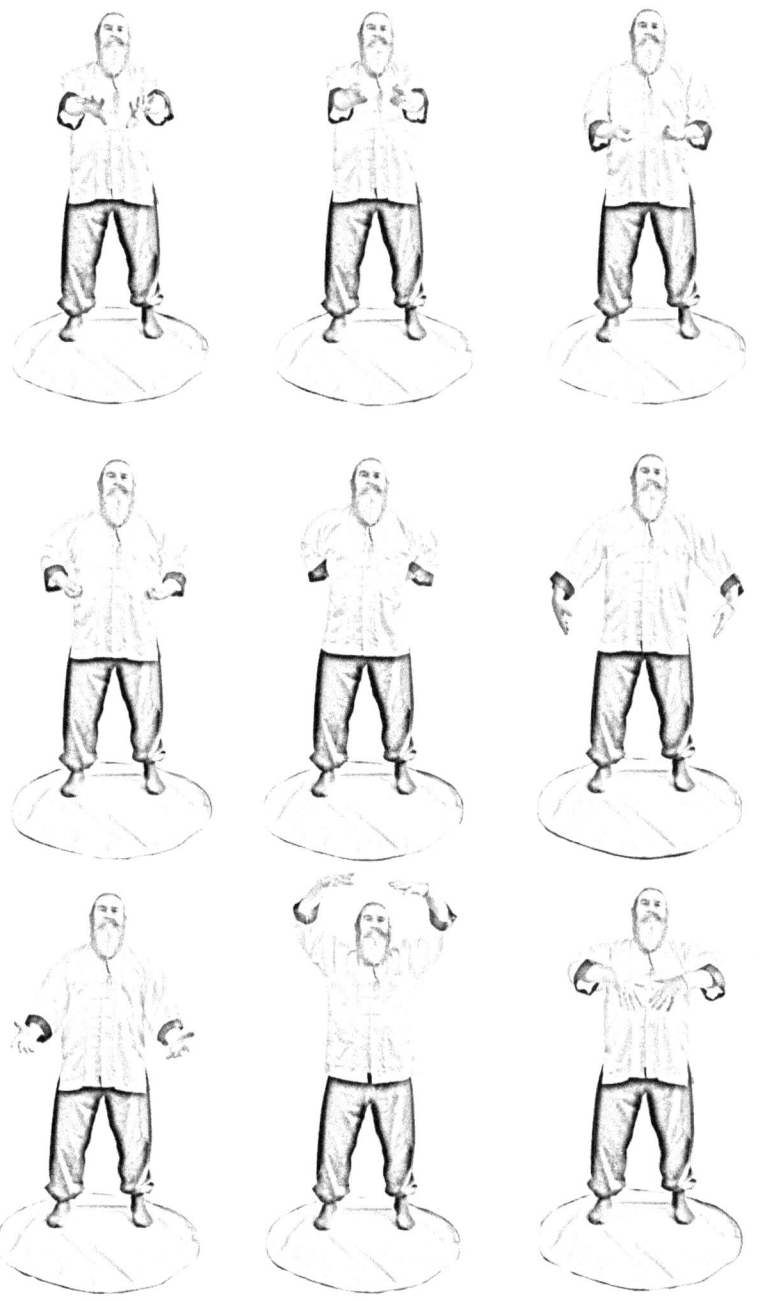

1b Connect to Umbilical region and spread energy Qi through the Dai Mai Belt Channel once more. Move hands behind back and rub Kidneys 3 times, then stand at ready, rise up & down- breath.

Dragon Fire Qigong

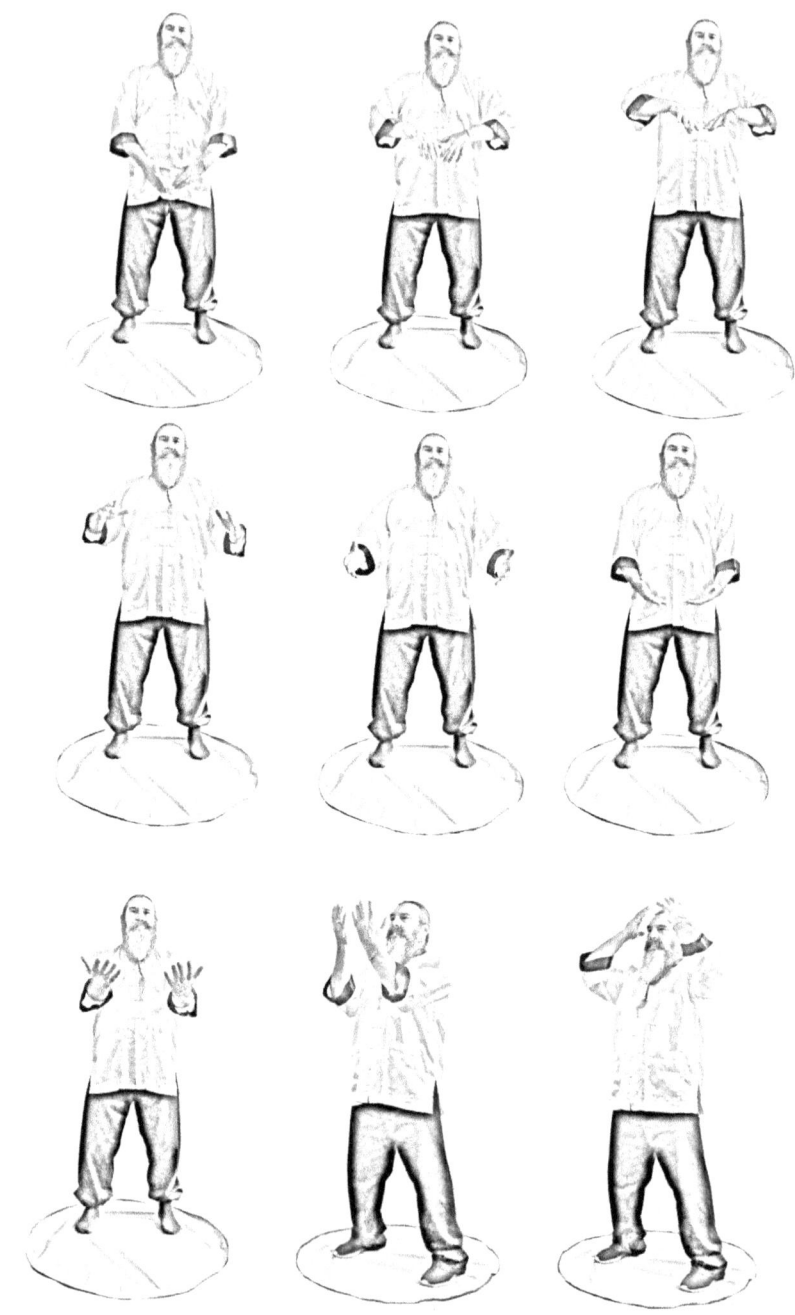

1c gather energy within belly region and bath the mind and brain
1d press energy of breath out and draw back positive energy to connect with downward press into Xia.

Meditations Harmony and Balanced Stretching

In Dragon Fire Qigong; I have designed the forms of Longevity, to correspond with the Soul Breath. This gives rise to the; fulfilling of blood harmony, is directed from within oxygenation, pressed into our body system and therefore, giving positive influence to growth and support for exercising.

1st, open breath sequence; this then leads into the intrinsic formulation of body Qi transformation, introduced through the umbilical press area, and circulation of the Dai Mai - Belt Channel.

Dragon Fire Qigong

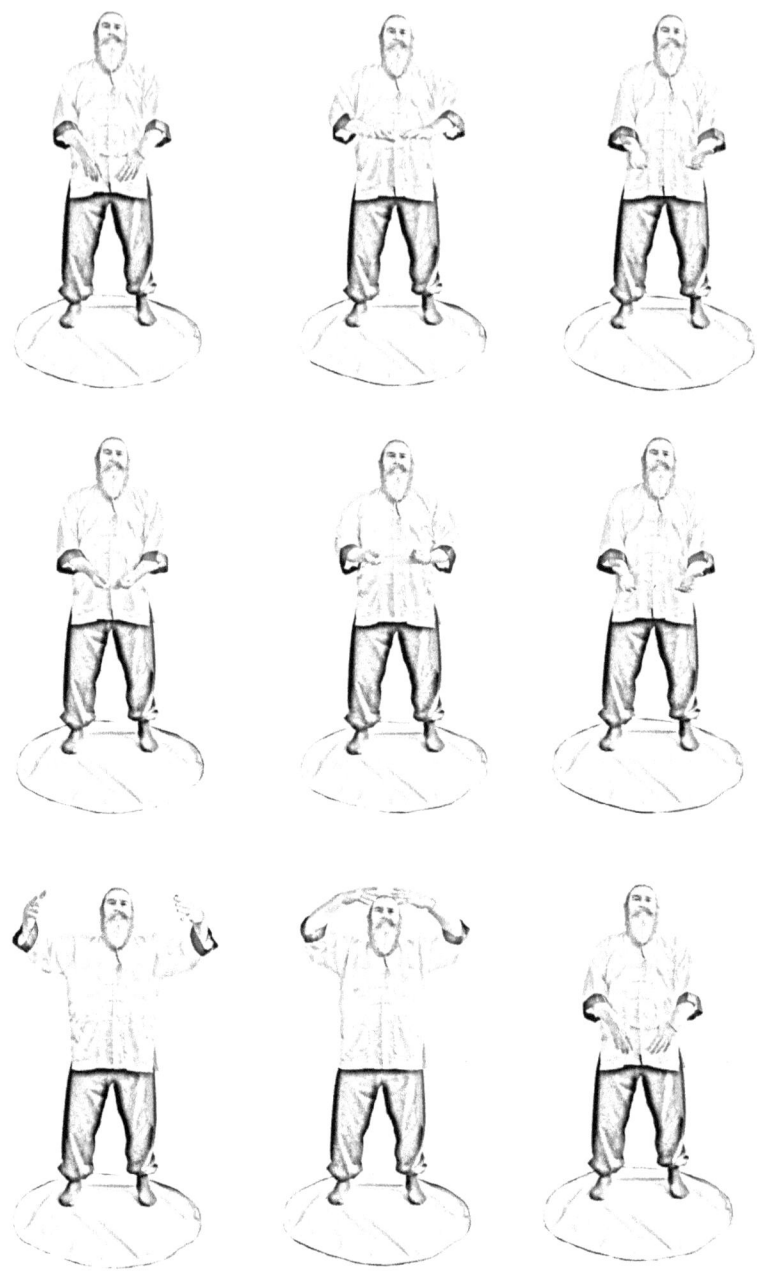

2nd. Represents both internal accumulation rises from Xia and also to represent the spirit of the self, formulates energy within the lower wellness centre. This performed 3 times, forming intrinsic development and corresponds with Dragon Fire Philosophy.

Meditations Harmony and Balanced Stretching

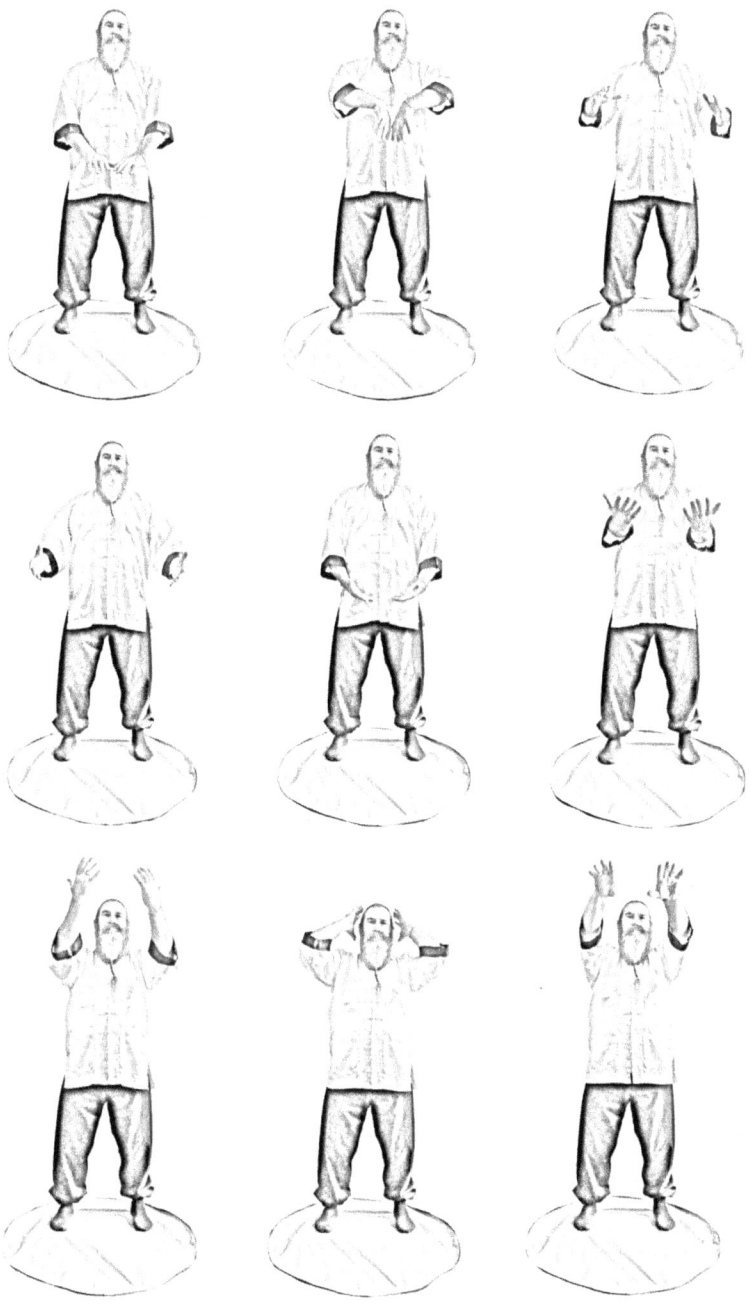

3rd Longevity circuit energies flow into our upper organ system; Heart and lungs. From our Earthly body organs; Stomach, Large Intestine, Small Intestine, Kidney; Spleen/Pancreas-Liver; ascend to 'Heaven' body organs, Heart-Lungs, after connecting from Xia.

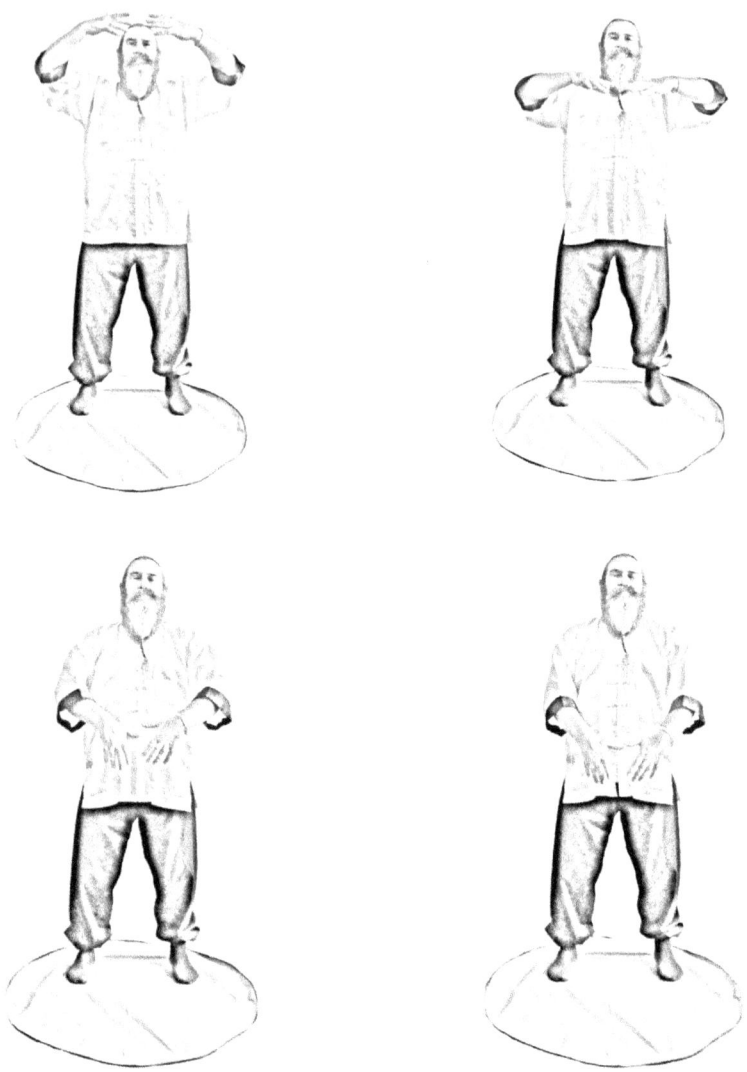

3rd Longevity circuit, ascends energy into our; Heart and lungs to infuse vitality from; Stomach, Large Intestine, Small Intestine, Kidney; Spleen/Pancreas-Liver; ascends to fill the 'Heaven' body organs- Heart-Lungs, after connecting through the body flow from Xia. Into our Mind- Brain region, connecting Laogong points in an Qi flow up to and around the Tai Yang (temples). This flow then releases heat outwards from the side of head, to release in a press out in front of the Shang; extended. Energy is then drawn back towards the Yin Tang point between the eyebrows, to connect positive energy from the universe, to then press downwards into the body Xia. This performed 3 times, forming intrinsic development and corresponds with Dragon Fire Philosophy.

Meditations Harmony and Balanced Stretching

4th stage is to take this repeating energy flow and step it out diagonally; first to the left side. In left forward stance facing left diagonal, your feet are pressed in readiness to create the flow of Qi and Blood energy, in synchronicity of the hands and arms moving.

Dragon Fire Qigong

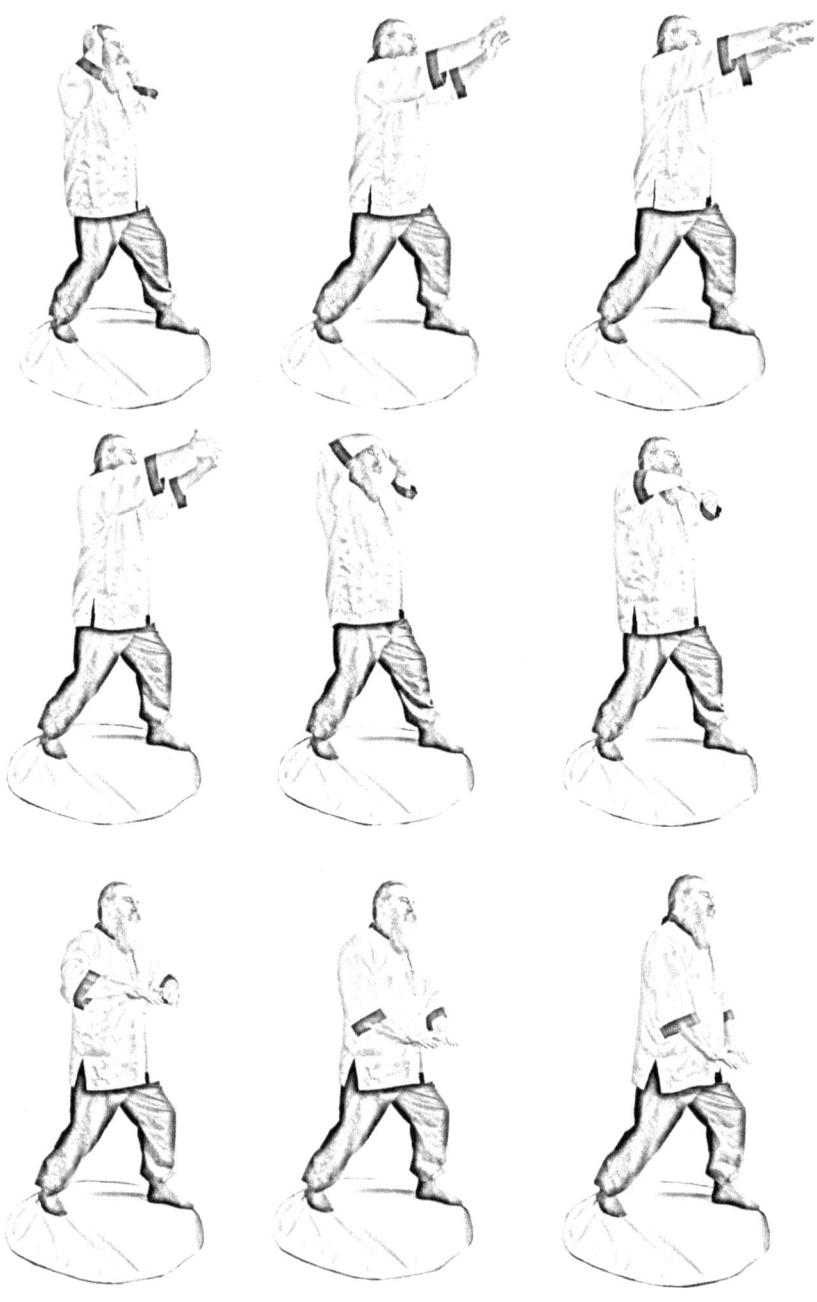

4a stage your intrinsic Qi formulations just gathered, are now delivering upwards to the Mind-brain, to once again press release, Tai Yang, then draw back into the Yin Tang. Press, descend through the core body central, into the legs.

Meditations Harmony and Balanced Stretching

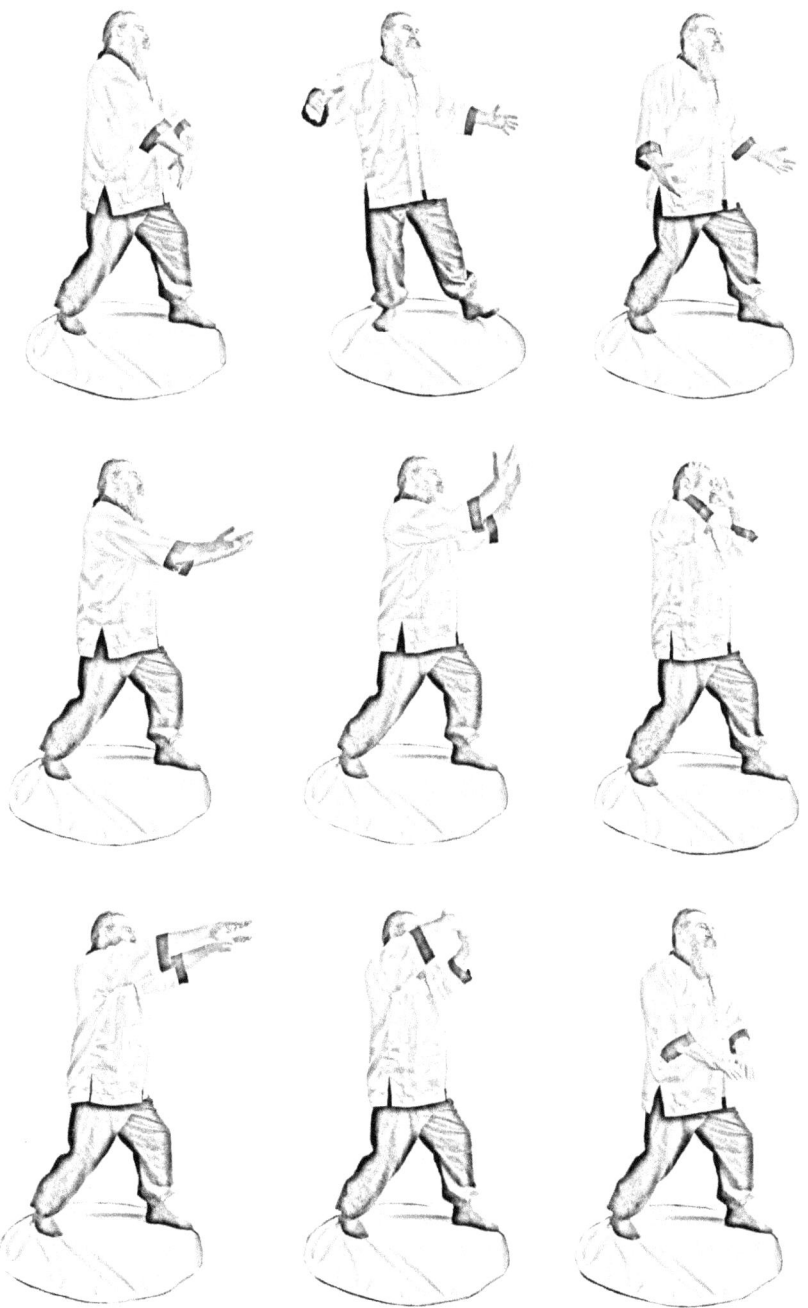

4ab stage your intrinsic Qi formulations are repeated, deliver to the Mind-brain, once again, Tai Yang, then draw back into the Yin Tang. Press, descend through the core, into the legs.

Dragon Fire Qigong

4b-c stage- After the flow of energy pressed through the legs, moves back and forth within the press and flow of arm, body, leg movements of Qi. Performed 3 times. This is then repeated to the right side, after a centring of energy flow to stabilise once more.

Meditations Harmony and Balanced Stretching

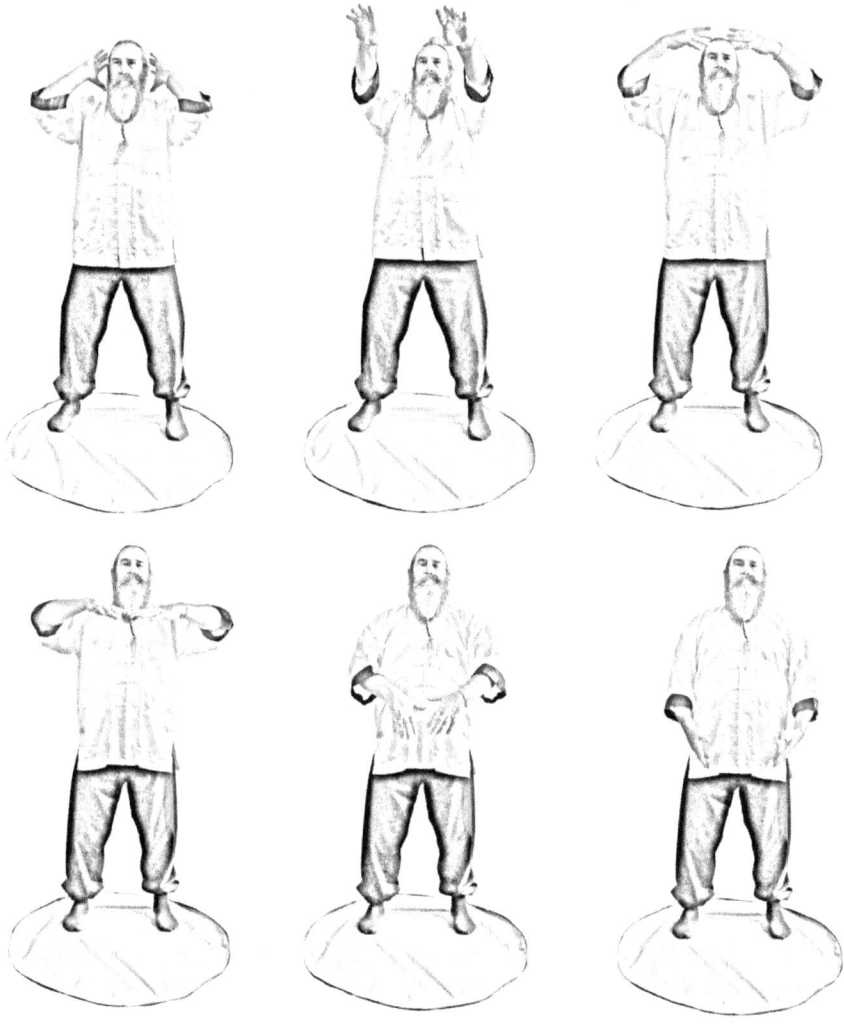

Designed to deliver smooth flowing and warming energy from bottom of the feet, up through the channels inside of legs. Then as you gather the intrinsic Qi energy of the lower Earth organs and Xia. Initiated from the pose of when standing after moving into diagonal, the palms facing up as if holding your intrinsic Qi formulations just gathered, are now delivering upwards to the Mind-brain, to once again press release, Tai Yang, then draw back into the Yin Tang. As you then descend through the press of Qi energy down to the inside middle left thigh. Connecting once more to the Blood energy from the legs. The flow of energy pressed through the legs, moves back and forth within the press and flow of arm, body, leg movements of Qi. This is then repeated to the right side, after a centring of energy flow to stabilise, then with an on flow affect, performed again diagonally through the arms and legs.

4th stage Right side; is to take this repeating energy flow and step it out diagonally. In Right forward stance facing, Right diagonal, your feet are pressed in readiness to create the flow of Qi and Blood energy, in synchronicity of the hands and arms moving.

Meditations Harmony and Balanced Stretching

4a stage your intrinsic Qi formulations just gathered, are now delivering upwards to the Mind-brain, to once again press release, Tai Yang, then draw back into the Yin Tang. Press, descend through the core body central, into the legs.

Dragon Fire Qigong

4b2 stage your intrinsic Qi formulations just gathered, are now delivering upwards to the Mind-brain, to once again press release, Tai Yang, then draw back into the Yin Tang. Press, descend through the core body central, into the legs.

Meditations Harmony and Balanced Stretching

4b2 stage- After the flow of energy pressed through the legs, moves back and forth within the press and flow of arm, body, leg movements of Qi. Performed 3 times. This is then centred once more, as an energy flow.

Dragon Fire Qigong

4c stage- After the flow of energy pressed through the legs, moves back and forth within the press and flow of arm, body, leg movements of Qi. Performed 3 times. This is then centred once more, as an energy flow. To settle into stage **5**

Meditations Harmony and Balanced Stretching

Qi energy of the lower Earth organs and Xia. Initiated from the pose of when standing after moving into diagonal, the palms facing up as if holding your intrinsic Qi formulations just gathered, are now delivering upwards to the Mind-brain, to once again press release, Tai Yang, then draw back into the Yin Tang. As you then descend through the press of Qi energy down to the inside middle left thigh.

Connecting once more to the Blood energy from the legs.

The flow of energy pressed through the legs, moves back and forth within the press and flow of arm, body, leg movements of Qi. This is then when repeated to the right side, creates the overall embellishment of transformational intrinsic Qi. Has been moved through and absorbed by the complete body system, after a centring of energy flow to stabilise, then prepare for the flow on affect.

Performed again horizontally through the arms and legs. Into the Eight Tri Gram connection of life building structures.

Dragon Fire Qigong

Centre once more to settle into stage **5;** To left side first then right side, extend through cloud hands, as feet extend outwards also forming middle Mountain stance.

Meditations Harmony and Balanced Stretching

Repeat into second extension of stage **5;** To left side first then right side, extend through cloud hands, as feet extend outwards also forming into middle Mountain stance Yang.

Dragon Fire Qigong

Press the Mountain Left-stage **6;** To left side first then swing horizontally right side, extend the Mountain Press through hands, formed as middle Mountain stance Yang. This leads to holding the Smoke-Lake, Spleen side blood flow.

Meditations Harmony and Balanced Stretching

From hold the Smoke-Lake to Form the Volcano stage **6a;** To left side first, arm upward. Then swing horizontally right side, Cloud-Wind movement of change. This leads to blood flow moving, Smoke-Lake, Spleen side blood flow.

Dragon Fire Qigong

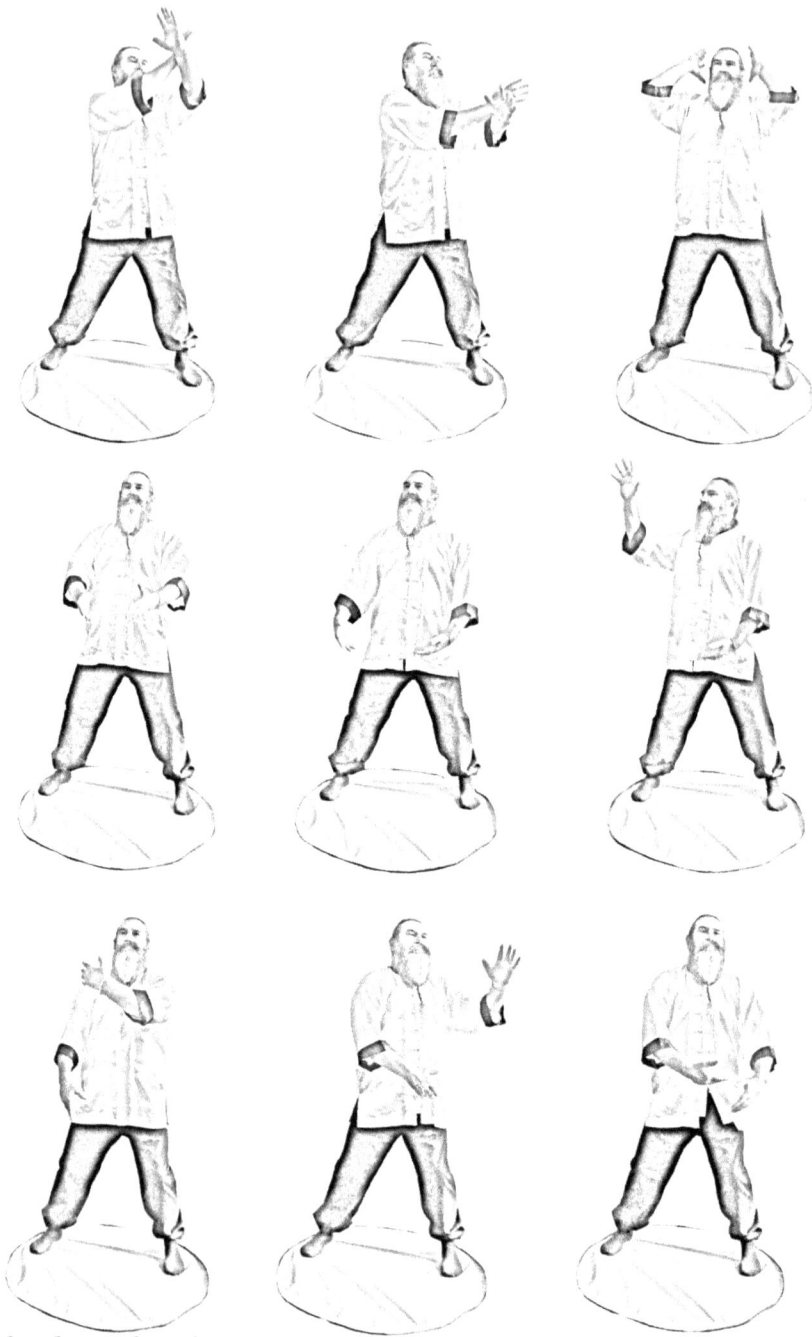

Cloud-Wind settles into Hands Through Clouds, stage **6b;** To Right side first, arm upward. Then Move Hands Through Clouds, Central movement of change. This leads to Qi blood flow centring, blood flow and Blood system harmony.

Meditations Harmony and Balanced Stretching

Hands Through Clouds, to Mountain Press- stage **6c;** To Right side first, Press the Mountain, then swing horizontally right to Left side, extend the Mountain Press through hands, formed as middle Mountain stance Yang leads to Qi blood flow centring,

Dragon Fire Qigong

Mountain Press- stage **6d;** From Left side continue, Press the Mountain, swing horizontally back to Right, extended Mountain Press through hands, Mountain stance Yang Holds the Lake (kidney-Liver) life energy- Dragon, into thunder and cloud wind.

Meditations Harmony and Balanced Stretching

Cloud-Wind settles into stage **6e;** Through the Left side To Right side swing arms upwards and around. Central movement of change. This leads to Qi blood flow centring, blood flow and Blood system harmony.

Settles into stage **6f;** Centring movement. This leads to Qi blood flow centring, blood flow and Blood system harmony. Movement through legs brings body back to starting place. Repeat all forms.

Meditations Harmony and Balanced Stretching

Dragon Fire Qigong

SECTION V:

BA DUAN JIN (SEATED METHOD) ESSENCE

BA DUAN JIN (SEATED METHOD) ESSENCE
Dragon Fire Qigong

Chapter 1 :

Ba Duan Jin; is a term for a system of eight movements or deliveries of practice excersise, in this case seated Qigong variations. It originally started with the sense of doing a basic standing formula, of some eight activities, to maintain general health and fitness for the populous in China. It, in this form is to represent that eight structured activities, are employed to bring energy forging and balance into the body spine, through the delivery of these simple techniques. Its main function is to connect the natural energy that ascend the spine around the head and descend once more in front of the spine/body.

This is the microcosmic orbit development. It is deemed as a way in which to enrich the spinal juices (Gu sui) and incorporate structural change into the marrow and into the body, connecting with major vital organs along the visceral system, thus bring calming thought via the sympathetic and para- sympathetic nerves. This fusion of Qigong connects both Gu Sui and Nao Sui, enriched spine and brain essences into the forging from flow on movements.

Transition of this particular form, which was first taught to the teacher 'Simon Blow Qigong' Sydney: in China; from "Grand Master Zong Yunlong of Wudang Mountain China." Grand Master Zong is one of the main Daoist Monks from the Purple Cloud Temple. Was he himself taught and then certified others to teach. As now is Simon!
     Being trained; Simon then trained me (as well as many others in his teachers trainer school) his style and techniques into this readiness of harmony training for Microcosmic Orbit. As my own style and physical preferences to energy differ from what 'Simon' had been taught, and delivers through himself into his structure of performing; "Absorbing the Essence" and "Wudang Longevity."
     I had personal difficulties due to spine and brain injuries.
     I have maintained my individual assessing of forms and incorporated other technical variations to deliver a more Yin essence (Gu Sui) formulation, in line with others forms I have witnessed. My style incorporates added ability for people whom have physical blockages or are elder and more frail, can also perform into finding harmony balanced through the Microcosmic Orbit [choosing of two pathways complimented in form] into my system of Qigong 'Dragon fire'.
     I must note that I had also referenced the training platform that Simons master had performed, forging theirs; as seen on video and in book forms revealed through others. Warming the spine extra circulation actions, then grew a more balanced style that I personify in Dragon Fire. My own adaptions of 'Longevity forms' energy of Spirit-Blood; and in line with Dragon Fire Qigong.

Meditations Harmony and Balanced Stretching

Preparation:

This style of Qigong/Nei gong is done in a seated position, either on a chair (back straight, seated on the near edge) or seated cross-legged upon a cushion or mat. Palms are placed down upon the knees. Performed after the 'Longevity forms', warming spirit- blood.

The eyes are closed, the chin tucked in, and the head is held as though an intention of thought is drawing you up through the Baihui point to straighten your spine further and to allow the energy a smoother transition around the body circuit. Place the tip of your tongue on the top of the palate just behind the teeth, yet relaxed. Breathe in through your nose naturally, in a relaxed state, and allow your mind to become calm.

Meditate on these three energy centres for a few minutes, starting with the Huiyin, then Baihui, and then concentrate on the Xia- wellness centre.

As you breathe in, allow the Qi to rise up the back along "Du Mai," starting from the base of your spine (sacrum) along the points of your energy channel, to the Baihui point, then over your head to Shang and then under into your upper lip, a point just below the nose.

From here, the energy focus is on your out-breath, from the middle of your lower lip, down the front of your body "Ren Mai," into the Xia- then onwards to Huiyin, completing a circle of this inner energy.

Use one breath to settle, before doing the breathing pattern called **circulation breath**, which is then done three times between each main section of the seated Ba Duan Jin.

Begin first through: Initiate Spirit; the sparkling eyes, then perform the sacral pump of Dragon Fire.

Open eyes to look with sparkle; with a sense of from your inner smile, move your eyes to see. Firstly, look up, then down; moving only your eyes for a count of twelve times (up and down count as one). Then look with sparkle; horizontally-left to right 12 times. Then in a diagonal; starting from left top-down to right. Then right top, down to left 12 times each side. Then circle your eyes; firstly, from left to right 9 times, then reverse right to left 9 times, before pausing with eyes clamped shut, then opening, to shut and open 9 times.
    Sitting on the chair edge or near front of chair or if on a cushion? 'Warm the sacrum with dragon spirals', nine circles pressing through the sitting bones and with hands focused into the Kua, as if holding a Qi ball, right to left in a figure 8 movement.

Then bring this warmed energy through your hands up the front spine, to the head; connect palm energy onto Shang (upper wellness centre)- middle forehead, with palms then moving out to temples, then draw the Qi downwards from face to chest down onto knees. Rest.

Breathe; then take two circulation Breaths.

The Waterfall from the Mountain - baths within.

This exercise stimulates both Du Mai and Ren Mai and warms Ming Men and the spine, opens and closes the cranial and sacral pumps interacting with the uniformity of macrocosmic actions and brings the para- sympathetic nervous system into play. Thusly; making the 'Gu Sui-marrow' more enriched and fluid; or as a saying, the spine becomes more juicy with 'Jing Qi' energy (Marrow).

Breathe in; then on the out-breath focus the intention to expel the breath as you arch your back inwards with your head moving forwards towards your knees. Then, as you begin your in-breath - rise with your back arching upwards and the reverse, to bring your trunk back to your starting position like a rolling flow. Do this movement as if you are bathing in a Waterfall to cleanse your; Head, Back, Face, and Chest.
    Repeat Six times: with a calming breath pause in-between the movements, before completing the sequence again. Breathing too deeply may increase the dizziness sensation- too much oxygenation into the blood, so remember to pause between the movements.

Breathe; then take two circulation Breaths.

Ba Duan Jin seated method Essence

Section One: Dragon Bites 36 Times

With the mouth closed, slowly clench the teeth in a biting fashion, clearly and deliberately 36 times. Remember not too hard and with your tongue gently placed behind upper teeth on the pallet. Keep a steady pace uniformly biting down and raising up. When these 36 bites have been done. The energy of the pallet and mouth enacting biting, forms a well of saliva in the bottom of the mouth, this is called the Dragons pool, enriched saliva that is swallowed down representing the merging of the mouth within meditations, connects to the stomach forging into the body a golden elixir enriched within.

Breathe; then take three circulation Breaths.

Meditations Harmony and Balanced Stretching

**Sparkling Eyes; Sacral Pump; Waterfall Baths Within;
Section One- Dragon Bites 36 times.**

Section Two A: Holding Kun Lun.

Kun Lun; refers to a sacred Mountain in China and is referenced here as the energy point at the back of the head, below is Yuzhen (jade pillow) and above is Feng fu (wind palace). This exercise helps stimulate the Heart and the Du Mai. Breathe in, bring hands up to the Kun Lun and interlock your left hand and your right hand held horizontally, elbows up shoulders back. At the same time, bring your Qi to the Baihui. Breathe out and send the Qi down to the Xia, as you bring your elbows toward your head and bend down in front of your body. Remember to keep energy of your arms soft and light. Let the energy press inwards at the elbows on the bend; the forge should be felt in the midriff front and on the back Jiaji, beginning of lower spine-rib cage region.

Whilst expelling air, you gently tense your abdomen and at the endpoint, if you wish-your anus (Huiyin). Done to seal in this Qi energy, before rising up with your breath to begin again. Go as far as is comfortable as you are only to stretch into your diaphragm-abdomen in your downward press.

It is not about force but making 'Gu Sui' active in movement (juice the spine). Repeat 9 times with a pause in between each breath cycle in-out.

To complete after the ninth press, you bring your hands up, over and down the front of face and body, to rest hands on the knees.

Breathe; then take three circulation Breaths.

Meditations Harmony and Balanced Stretching

Section 2 A: Holding Kun Lun

Dragon Fire Qigong

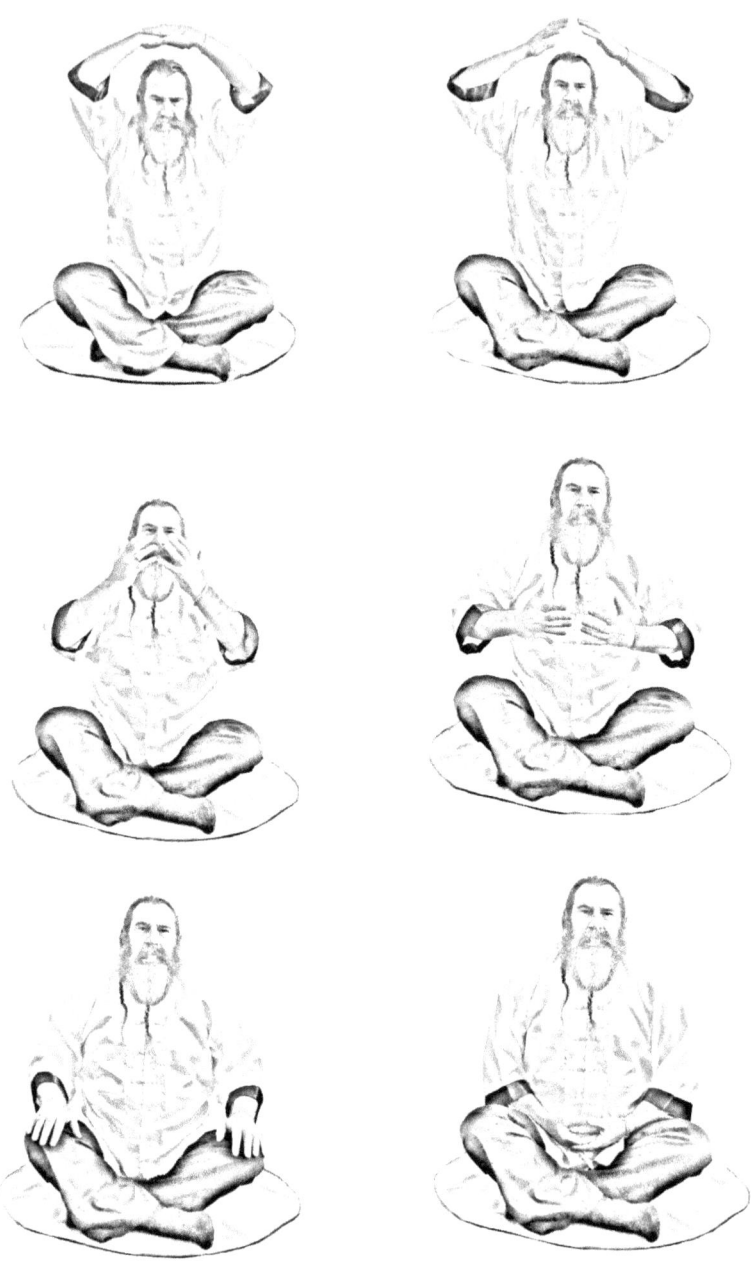

Section 2A: Settling

Section Two B: Strum the Brain like a heavenly Drum.

This exercise helps stimulate the Heart and Du Mai and stimulates the Nao Sui of the Brain- Cerebellum (Feng Fu) in connection to the juice that rises up with the spine marrow into the brain. Breathe in and bring your hands over your ears with your palms pressing like a cupping action, to seal the eardrums. At the same time Qi is taken to the Bai Hui. Then breathe out, taking the Qi to Xia. With fingers spread onto the back of head 'Cerebellum' Feng Fu, and-Yuzhen Jade cushion, and your thumbs pressed onto your neck and under your rear jaw.

Begin to strum your fingers to a count of twenty-four. Pull your palms out from your ears, releasing the cupping before drawing hands down the front of face, neck, forwards onto your upper chest, then your upper thighs to your knees.

Breathe; Repeat three times.

After three circuits.

Breathe; then take three circulation Breaths.

Section 2B: Strum the Brain like a Heavenly Drum

Then Settle again.

Section Three: Stretch the Mountain Peaks.

This exercise stimulates the Heart; Ming Men and Du Mai, reinforces the spine- muscles and back. Fills Qi into the chest and lungs and brings kidney Jing to the Heart and lungs. Breathe in; bring the hands to the back of your head (Kun Lun). At the same time, take the Qi to Baihui. Breathe out as your Qi is bought down to Xia, pause with one breath; before recommencing.

Breathe out; turn the head to the left, twisting through the spine, taking care to only twist as far as comfortable, keep your elbows slightly toward so as not to put to much strain on your neck and shoulders.

Feel the breath squeeze out within the central core- solar plexus; also called the celiac plexus- this complex system of radiating nerves and ganglia, is found in the pit of the stomach, in front of the Aorta. It is part of the sympathetic nervous system. Playing an important role or function in our body connects to stomach, kidneys, liver and adrenal glands and abdomen.

Breathe in, rotating the body back to the front. Repeat this sequence twenty four times to the left. Bring palms to your knees. Rest for a few breaths.
    Then repeat on the right side twenty four times. When finished, place palms on knees. Relax and feel the essence within.

Breathe; then take three circulation Breaths.

Meditations Harmony and Balanced Stretching

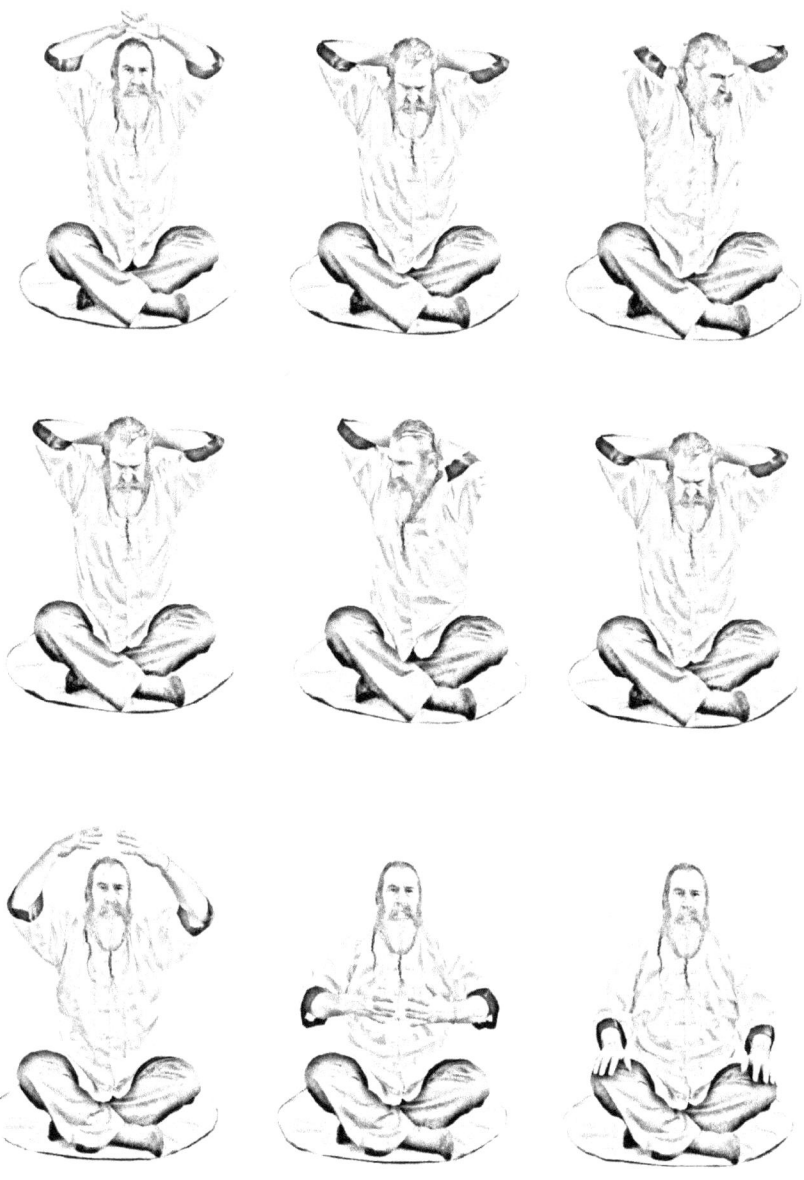

Section 3: Stretch the Mountain Peaks

Section Four: Red Dragon Swims in the Golden Pool.

This excersise connects the nourish in Ren mai in a sense; a connection of which develops as an aid too, and within the digestive system. It also is an important prerequisite to establishing deeper Nei Dan elixir meditation abilities to forming the golden elixir.
	Rotate the tongue in one direction around the inside of the teeth and gums in a circular motion upon the inner gums as if sucking, building up rich saliva or our Golden nectar (charged with Qi).

Do this 18 times, then continuing 18 times in the reverse direction before swimming the tongue around within this enriched fluid, then swallowing down with a gulping sound; giving you the Yang energy of 36 movements.

Breathe; then take three circulation Breaths.

Section Five: Warming the Kidney House.

This exercise helps stimulate the Kidneys. Rub the hands together; then with your top hand moving in a circle over your other palm press the rub massage, then turn over and repeat the rubbing hands. Creating the inner fire in Laogong, of which to then rub onto your Kidneys, by firstly holding your warmed palms onto the kidney region of the Ming Men. And then rubbing your finger tips and palms upwards and around 36 times in circles into the lower back, this to infuse energy into your Ming Men (kidney house). Then allow the kidneys to absorb the warmth again through your palms pressed. Place hands back onto knees.

Breathe; then take three circulation Breaths.

Meditations Harmony and Balanced Stretching

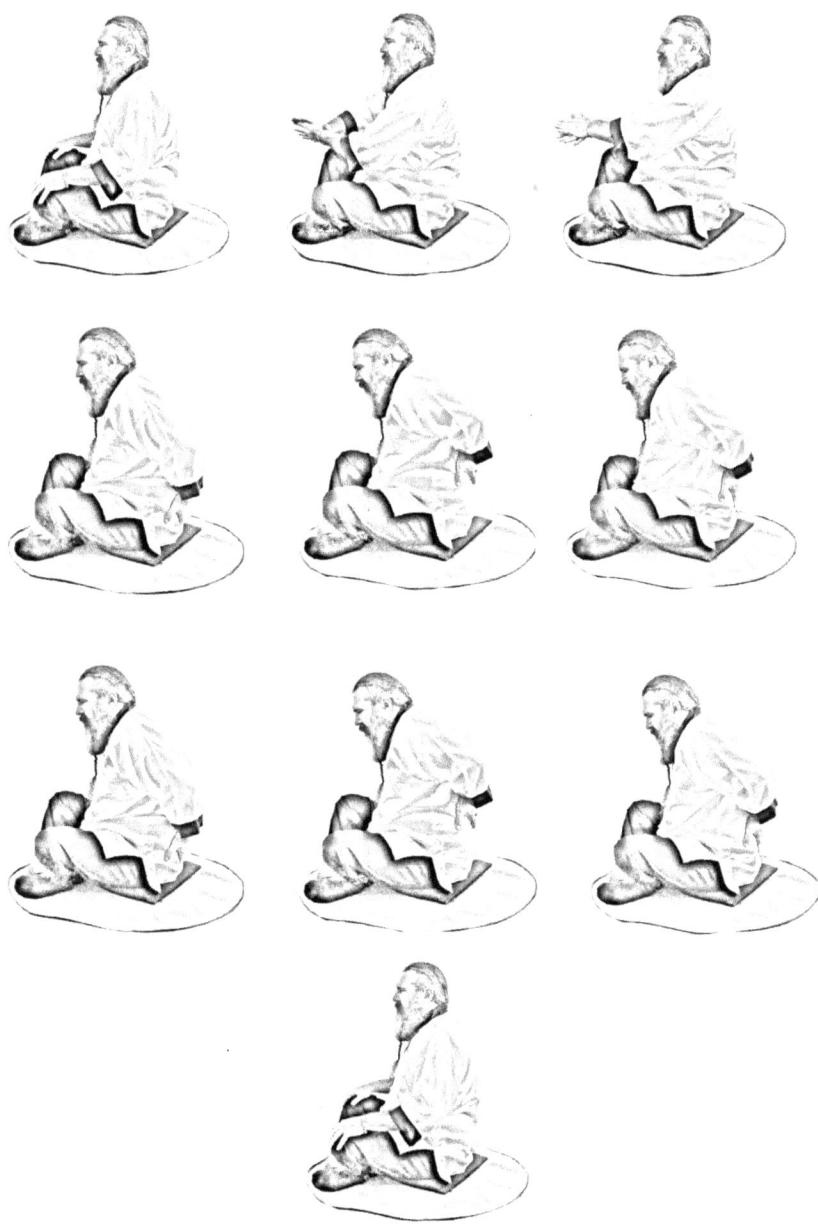

**Section 4-5: Red Dragon Swims in the Golden Pool;
Warming the Kidney House.**

Section Six A: Turning Water Wheel both sides.

This exercise helps stimulate the five Yin organs - Heart, Spleen, Lungs, Kidneys, and Liver. Place both palms face up at the level of Xia. Breathe in, as you bring the right hand tracing kidney meridian to the upper chest-mouth, with the mind-breath rising up the spine to Feng Fu (Cerebellum), then circle out in front with hand fingers pointing upwards, looking across fingertips. As we breathe out, we lower our hand back down in a circling effort, to our starting position- settled in Xia. Starting on the right side brings the parasympathetic nervous system into play.
    This is the Dragons harmony in Dragon Fire 'of water element feeds the liver system' onto heart and lungs.
    The cerebellum is the working connect of brain- mind performs onto our body movement platform.

Pause for a few relaxed breaths; then repeat with your left hand performing the sequence. The left hand connects the sympathetic nervous system (central spine; T-1, L-2) Dazhui- Ming men; to the rising of Kidney-water element, feeds the Spleen, Lungs, Heart. It is the Tiger nourish- in of Dragon Fire and merges the activity of the cerebellum to our breath and spine formulations.

Breathe rising up through the spine to Feng Fu (Cerebellum). Breathing out, the hand goes up and down in a circle then up again (like turning a wheel). Drawing Qi elixir up from Kidneys Ming men, Xia and into the mouth on the in-breath, then swallow down this elixir (when saliva is built up), as your hand creates the wheel action; as the provision of water, essentially nourishing the body. Repeat Nine times each side.

Breathe; then take three circulation breaths.

Close by bringing your hands up to the level of Shang with an in-breath. Then exhaling with the palms pressing Qi energy down towards the Xia before resting hands on your knees.

Breathe; then take three circulation Breaths.

Meditations Harmony and Balanced Stretching

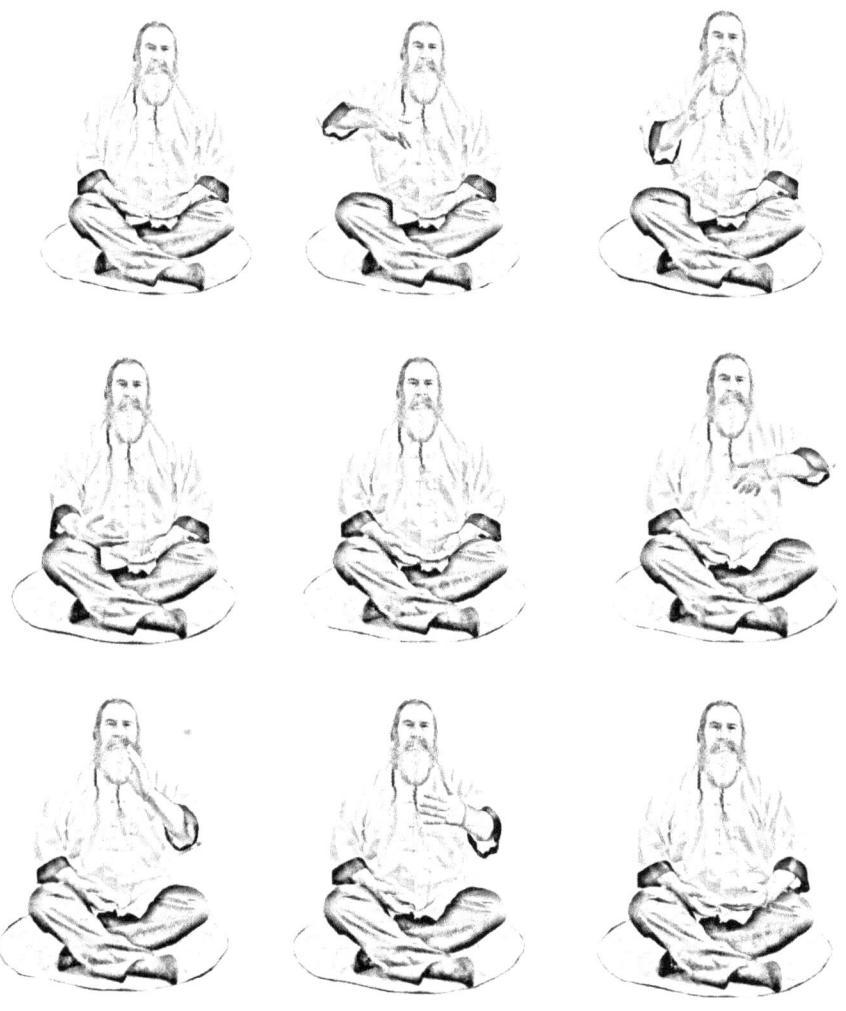

Section 6A: Turning the Water Wheel both sides

Section Six B: Turning the Water Wheel both hands.

This stimulates the five Yin organs. Place palms face up at the Xia. Breathe in and bring both hands tracing up Kidney Meridian into upper chest-mouth height, then rotate hands fingers from downwards facing first, into fingers pointing up as an action of turning like a Wheel-Pump. Breathe out, bring hands around forwards and down in a semi-circle action. When breathing in, bring the Qi up the back to the Kun Lun point (Cerebellum) as your Hands and fingers direct the energy upwards through the kidney Meridian; turning fingers to move to point up as your begin to circle into your descent, feel this energy Qi pass from Kun Lun to the mouth. And remember when breathing out, move the Qi down the arms to the hands and fingers. Pause in Xia; and if choosing too, add a gentle upward squeeze through Hui Yin before ascending with breath once more.

This is the combined harmony of your motor- brain and nervous systems interacting with the intrinsic water element flow of Microcosmic orbiting. Repeat Nine times.

Close by bringing your hands up to the level of Shang with an in-breath. Then exhaling with the palms pressing Qi energy down towards the Xia before resting hands on your knees.

Breathe; then take three circulation Breaths.

Meditations Harmony and Balanced Stretching

Section 6B: Turning Water Wheel Both Hands

Section Seven: Tapping the Roof.

This exercise helps stimulate Qi through all the channels. When using formulations of awareness training, Men start with: Breathe in, raise both hands up in front of the throat and face, with your inside left wrist (little finger) Heart 6 point; touching inside of your outside hand- right wrist (thumb) Lung 7 point, formed like an X. Then draw up and over onto the top of your head, if a male; with the left hand placed on top of your right, both hands pressing down to touch your Baihui. Then, in a sequence of lifting hands up and then tapping with gentle firmness onto the top of your head, with tongue placed gently behind the teeth on top of your palate (therefore tapping the roof), in order to stimulate the body and spine and pressing Brain energy 'Nao Sui' into the Hypothalamus.

Repeat the tapping Nine times. Remember this; when you bring both of your hands up at the same time with an in-breath, bring the Qi up your back to the Baihui- pause. The left to right formulations is the connecting of Yang energy male forms into the pulse-blood Xue from left wrist Heart, Liver, Kidney channel. Blood returns spirit. Pulse- Blood and Meridians derived pathways. When done as a **Female**:Breathe in, raise both hands up in front of the throat and face, with your inside right wrist (little finger) Heart 6 point; touching inside of your outside hand- left wrist (thumb) Lung 7 point, formed like an X. Then draw up and over onto the top of your head, if a female; with the right hand placed on top of your left, both hands pressing down to touch your Baihui. This then makes contact with the pulse of Nourish-in soul breath of the Tiger; Lungs, Spleen, pericardium. With the right hand being on top of left for the tapping movements. Do the tapping with relaxed natural breathing.

Then breathe out, as your hands press the Qi down through the Ren Mai, in front of your body - into your Xia, and then place hands onto your knees. Repeat this sequence three times. Then relax and feel within; with your hands returned to the knees. If choosing too, alternate between both blood circuits, remembering which starts- Male or female also ends as. This sequence is performed to show awareness of the difference between female 'Blood- Qi Xue' energy and 'Male Blood' directions. Done within an awareness training format. Similar to when resting in Xia; males have right hand on top of left, and females have left hand on top of right. Male energy, Dragon is stored in the Liver, but nourished by Tiger, female- Spleen/Stomach and Lungs system, and female 'Blood' energy settles in the body and supplies the growing 'foetus' in support from the liver. As in females; support of the Uterus and Chong Mai (Qihai) blood energy differs. As with Dragon Fire Qigongs completing awareness of the connecting sequenced forms and theory, through formulations of TCM training in Qigong. Yuan Qi, is Kidneys based, supports the Blood being.

Breathe; then take three circulation Breaths.

Meditations Harmony and Balanced Stretching

Section 7: Tapping the Roof (Male)

Dragon Fire Qigong

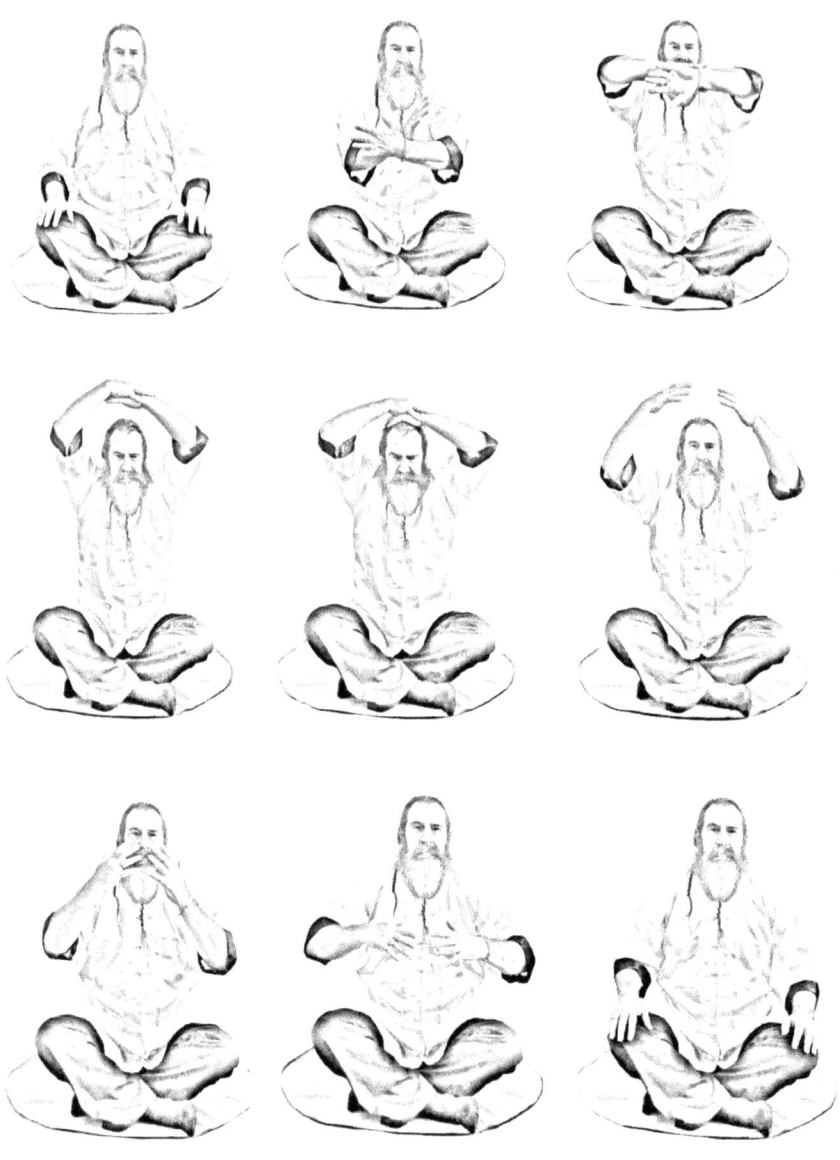

Section 7: Tapping the Roof- Female

Section Eight: Dragon stretches into Yongquan.

This exercise will stimulate Qi down, and up the legs. If you are sitting on the floor, place both legs out in front, slowly. Allow the blood to circulate through the legs with a massage, firstly at the Weizhong point (behind knee), then Stomach 36 allowing build up of energy to dissipate down the outside of your thighs and legs, then upwards through the inside of your legs and thighs. Once the warming has been sensed in your legs; reach down and hold your feet, as you press your fingers into the Yongquan points, with a massage.

Do a slow system massage of Qi energy down the outside of hips and legs without touching, pausing to press into yongquan point with finger tips. Then bring hands to outside of feet and draw energy back up your legs to hips without touching. Do this Qi massage 11 times in a circuit

But if you are sitting on a chair; stretch your legs out, with your toes up and the heels touching the surface. Then complete the sequence of massage into Weizhong (bladder 40) behind knee; and stomach 36 (Zusanli) four finger widths on the centre outside line of leg beneath the knee region. Do this to release energy build up before tracing a Qi massage down your hips and legs, but without touching your body, as a scan of energy passes down your legs into your feet. When feet are reached, you then press your Yongquan point (Kidney 1) the point behind the ball of your foot. Release; then draw energy back up with your hands from outside your feet-legs, still not touching until you reach your hips, to then repeat circuit a total of 11 times.

If you can't reach your feet, hold your ankles, pause. Finish by rubbing; first by lifting foot up into lap and then massaging the Yongquan point on the sole of each foot. Then return legs back to the position for meditation, with hands on knees. Take two circulation breaths.

When finished; we enter a quiet, peaceful space, and meditate for as long as feels comfortable- three to five minutes is a good starter- (or a period of twenty minutes; is a greater proficiency of this ability?).

Allow your Qi to merge with the universe, thus returning to your Spirit/Self.

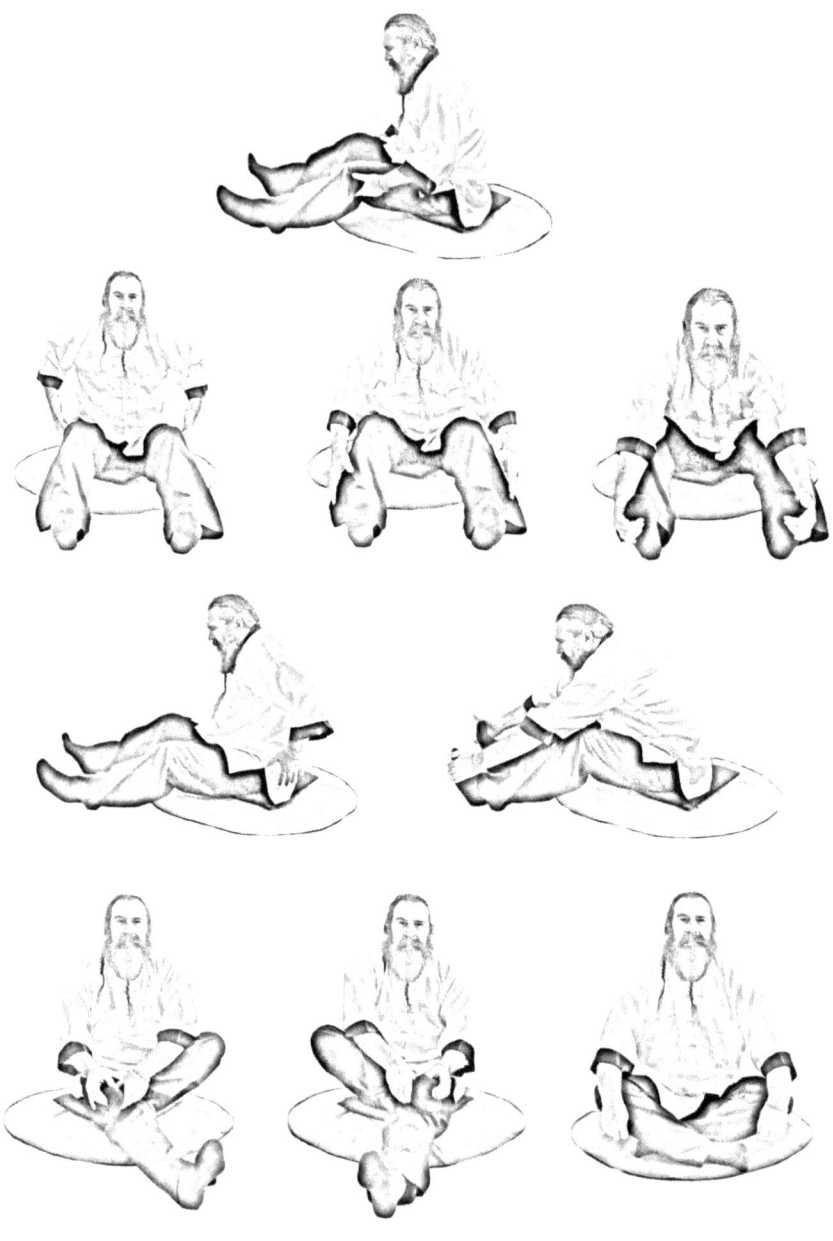

Section 8: Dragon Stretches into YongQuan

Meditations Harmony and Balanced Stretching

Dragon Fire Qigong

Meditations Harmony and Balanced Stretching

SECTION VI:

THREE LOCKS for MEDITATION

Chapter 1:

The Three Locks for Meditation

The Three Locks: The three locks are used to create a therapeutic compression within the abdominal cavity, to give a strong boost to the venal circulation, open the meridians and help activate the pneumogastric- (of or relating to Lungs and stomach) nerves of the parasympathetic (originates in the Brain stem and lower spine) branch of the autonomous nervous system. "Anal Lock- Abdominal Lock-Neck Lock." The locks are applied at or toward the end of inhalation, held in place briefly during compression, and released on exhalation.

The Anal Lock: is designed to lift the entire pelvic floor, in order to lock in, and enhance, the compression, created in the abdominal cavity by the diaphragm, as it descends from above during inhalation. The pelvic floor also known as the "urogenital diaphragm," consists of a flexible web of muscle, and tendon, that supports the colon, prostrate, uterus and sacral glands. By flexing this lower diaphragm, the anal lock massages all of the organs and glands within the sacrum. Strengthens the tissues of the pelvic floor, and gives stimulation to the sacral roots of the pneumogastric nerve endings. Which helps activate the immune response of the parasympathetic nervous system. As inhalation approaches completion, the anal lock is applied by contracting the outer ring of the anal sphincter. This manoeuvre lifts the anus and contracts the webbing of the entire urogenital diaphragm. For more powerful effect it may be extended deeper into the anus, this raises the Perineum, "Huiyin" between the anus and the sexual organs, and deepens the compression throughout the sacrum.

The Abdominal Lock:
The purpose of the abdominal lock is to seal in the therapeutic compression in the abdominal cavity, when the diaphragm descends, and the pelvic floor is raised with the anal lock- on completion of inhalation. To apply the abdominal lock, simply pull the lower part of the abdominal wall inward towards the spine. It is neither necessary nor desirable to pull it in too far, or with effort. Just draw in slightly with a light contraction, and hold briefly. Then relax completely-when exhaling.

The Neck Lock: serves several functions. By partially constricting the carotid arteries in the throat, it prevents excess blood from rushing straight up into the brain due to enhanced circulatory pressure from below. The Neck lock seals the breath down in the lungs after inhalation, and stretches the entire spinal cord from skull to sacrum, stimulating all the nerves and ganglia and opening energy channels that run along the spine.

To apply the neck lock, wait until the anal and abdominal locks are in place, then gently contract the throat muscles. Simply tucking the chin in without moving the neck much, and stretching the back of neck. Simply raise the chin when ready to exhale, relax and let the air flow out. To make it work in unison, is to do it all in one movement, as a gentle relaxed flow.

The Four stages of Qigong Breath control: The four stages of breath control are; inhalation, compression, exhalation, and intermission. In practice these four stages are strung together in a smooth continuous sequence, like the rise and fall of waves, or ripples on a lake, with each one playing a particular role and all of them connecting through the diaphragm.

Inhalation: With empty lungs and nostrils flared, relax the diaphragm and commence a slow, smooth inhalation through the nose, deliberately drawing the air deep down into the bottom of the lungs-so that the diaphragm descends and the abdominal wall expands. As you continue to fill the lungs, and the ribcage and abdomen have expanded- hold the breath within. A full breath in Qigong is about 2/3rds to 3/4s full, with most of the air packed down into the lower and middle of the lungs, as to expand the abdominal wall.

Compression: This phase is quite brief-usually only around three seconds- but its benefits are deep and multiple. The first step of the compression stage is to press the diaphragm firmly downward, to settle air into the bottom of the lungs and the abdominal cavity. As you do this apply the **"three locks"**- the three locks are used to create a therapeutic compression, to give a strong boost to the venal circulation, open the meridians and help activate the pneumogastric- (of or relating to Lungs and stomach) nerves of the parasympathetic (originates in the Brain stem and lower spine) branch of the autonomous nervous system. "Anal Lock-Abdominal Lock-Neck Lock."

Now; when performed properly, this brief retention of breath, helps slow down and deepen the pulse of the heart and balance blood pressure throughout the circulatory system.

By increasing the pressure of air in the lungs, the blood is enriched with an extra supply of oxygen, and allows more elimination of carbon dioxide. Even the briefest breath retention triggers cellular respiration, an innate response that allows cells to breathe by themselves.

When this happens, blood sugar is spontaneously broken down by the cells, to release oxygen and produce body heat.

Never hold the compression phase of breath beyond what feels comfortable.

Exhalation: When you're ready to exhale. Release the three locks, relax the diaphragm and ribs, and begin exhaling slowly and evenly in a steady continuous flow through the nostrils or lips, depending on the exercise. Empty the lungs in reverse order, from the top of the lungs, then the middle, and bottom. Continue exhaling until lungs are empty, letting the abdominal wall contract inward and the diaphragm ascend upward into the chest.

Intermission: When the lungs are empty and exhalation is complete, do not immediately start drawing in another breath. Instead pause briefly to let the diaphragm and abdominal wall relax, and move back into place, ready for the next breath.

The above section **'Three Locks for Meditation':** *is derived from a book by Daniel P. Reid 1948.*
Chi Kung: Harnessing the power of the universe.

Meditations Harmony and Balanced Stretching

Dragon Fire Qigong

Meditations Harmony and Balanced Stretching

SECTION VII:

**UNDERSTANDING THE MENTAL
BODY**

Understanding the Mental Body

Mind; the third part of the human body, the mental or spiritual body. First, let's consider the difference between the Mental and the Spiritual. Even with today's broader systems of knowledge and science. A difficulty in defining these two aspects of our nature, creates within itself a need to look back, at experiences gained in the past. In my past I knew that there is in me, a Spirit formed, outside my living body self, and represented; I also know that my living body 'Brain and Heart Xin' have a connection through thought and emotions.

According to the TCM understanding, our mental part includes both the physical and the Qi aspects within our being, that which are related to thinking. The physical parts being our nervous system and our brain, needing Qi to exist and function. If the physical brain and nervous system receive the right amount of Qi they stay healthy, the mind will think clearly and judge more wisely (sympathetic and para- sympathetic nervous system awareness).

However, Qi supply if not normal, will cause the brain and nervous system functions not to run properly, thus mental problems may occur. Naturally, if the Qi stops, the physical systems break down- we die. Therefore, in order to keep the mental system functioning properly, TCM- Qigong places emphasis on learning how to lead Qi to the brain to nourish it. Good Qigong also shows how to maintain our nervous system. When our mental aspects of physical being remain healthy, we also build up our spiritual part of our body.
    It is very difficult to understand and define this spiritual partnership; therefore, without the many trainings for awakening or awareness of something beyond the general aspects of body and mind. How can we then lead on to find "that which is ours" from within the perspective of becoming, in a greater sense more defined in the capabilities of generating mind in essence freed- to reveal. An enlightened state of mind, body, and breath (soul-breath). This is defined in my forms as "Dragon Fire." Delivery within us and along with the many forms; the mental part of our being can be considered a lower level of our spiritual sense, one which has not yet performed "Enlightenment" (in Daoism, called 'Shen Tong') beyond the living aspect of the lower level- living matter realm. We are seeing as such; now the spirit becomes and is that which is cultivated! Qi in the body will be able to combine and communicate with the Qi of Nature "Dao." Harmonious Self.
    This enables us to better understand the patterns of natural Qi; Spirit- Self and ultimately learn how to avoid what's deemed as rebirthing, or sliding back into the lesser worth of soul destructions, heavily prevalent in this earthly realm.

Meditations Harmony and Balanced Stretching

The mental part of our being is actually our thinking, which can be manifested externally. Intrusive thoughts or developed incisiveness; derived from external sources can build up an energy detrimental to our purpose, of finding- Calm, peace, or joyous feelings in a corrupt world or environment. As our brain has capacity to remember, store thoughts and be tied to the past? When these manifestations occur, a process is completed through the Qi circulatory and nervous systems. This means that the mind, Qi, and physical body cannot be separated; letting the possibility of stress back in.

In order to calm down the physical body, we must first calm the breath, and then calm the Qi body through the nervous system. Therefore, to enable this, we must first learn to regulate the mind 'in aid of our breath' which in-turn dissipates excess energies such as Anger, Anxiety, Stress compulsion or; Thought contention through depression (past), Anxiety (future). Pathways of delivery on the sympathetic and para- sympathetic nerves, highlights how these simple pathways to our complete connection of a physical beings harmony, can be disruptive. If you have ever hit a nerve, you would know just how painful and easy it is to hurt. By completing a simple yet needed pathway of learning meditative techniques, we can change; become like new, cleaned from within our heart and mind felt dilemmas.

Two Minds

Because of the close relationship between the mind, Qi, and physical body, regulating the mind is an important part of Qigong training. Chinese medicine and Qigong teach that there are two minds: one is called Xin, and the other is called Yi. The mind that is influenced by emotional disturbances is called Xin. Xin means "heart" in Chinese. Any event that can touch your heart and disturb your neutral mind, is considered Xin. For example, if you are upset because someone or something has treated you badly, the thoughts or intentions you have in response are considered Xin; and create that energy thought field, which is affecting the heart/mind. Our bodies organs in 'five element theory' reveal this construct in fullness. Types of thought included in each organs distribution to the heart energy, revolve around this necessity of function. Understand and be Aware.

In a different perspective, if you have scheduled Qigong training, but you feel too lazy and decide to skip it, the thought process leading to that decision is related to Xin. Xin can therefore be translated as the "emotional mind."

However, when thoughts arise from wise thinking and clear judgment, then they can be called the "mind of intent" or "Yi", connecting deeply to the mind's sense, even to the point where no verbal thought is needed to be transferred! An act of "Will-Yi" is therefore involved in the enactment of your Soul/Breath Defence. A particular aspect of Chi Boxing; Qigong, is practicing techniques to such a point, that no thought is required to execute them in self-defense; it becomes natural and decisive in reaction. Yet, when practiced with a deeper intent, you consciously emphasise directing the Qi - Yi, felt in the execution of the technique. In Qigong these forms of awareness trainings, become deeply ingrained in our consciousness and psyche.

Unfortunately, the emotional mind usually dominates over the wisdom mind in everyday thinking. Thus, when people react to events, it is often based on emotional feelings rather than calm judgment. That's being human.

One of the achievements of Qigong, is your development through the wisdom mind, so that it can better govern the emotional mind. When this occurs, emotional disturbances tend to happen less frequently and with less turbulence, allowing the mind to cultivate calmness in balanced harmony.

The emotional mind is considered Yang-inspired, while the wisdom mind is Yin. Qigong training aims to balance Yin and Yang. With this perspective, one can understand that the mental body is actually composed of "two minds." When either mind becomes too dominant and causes your actions to deviate from a neutral, balanced state, mental equilibrium is lost. This imbalance can also affect how your physical body functions.

Below: Qigong Meditation: Methods of Stopping intrusive Thought

Before you start, you should understand that there are no techniques that are absolutely effective for everybody. It depends on the individual. It may also depend on the situation and timing. Remember that the final goal of regulating your thoughts is to reach "the thought of no thought-serene calm." In other words, to regulate your thoughts without actively thinking about regulating them. Therefore, you must continue practicing until regulation happens naturally, and you do not need to consciously manage your thoughts. It is when you reach this stage you notice your mind to be free and neutral.

When a thought emerges, you should immediately recognise this is just a thought, it will pass just like a cloud in the sky passing. By developing awareness of what is happening, simply halt each new thought. This process is known as (stopping thought method).

You may find that as soon as you stop one thought, another arises immediately. You stop that one, but yet another pops up, seemingly without end. This leads onto the beginning method, return to the breath. Return to the breath is like the start position in any meditations beginning, relax, release the hold that this thought intrusion may have in your mind, remember it's just in your mind. To break this cycle; wait until your mind is clear, calm, and peaceful, and then position your mindful intent- Yi there, before any new thoughts arise from the heart-mind Xin. By keeping your mind in this neutral state, further thoughts will be prevented. The following are methods commonly used by meditators to prevent new thoughts from arising.

Generally, there are three steps to stopping greater intrusive thoughts:

Tie to the Origin and Stop Method: In this training, you bind your mind to one place, much like being tied to a position until you learn, what it is you needed. If you can keep your Yi centred at a specific point, you can control your emotive thoughts. This is done when your minds interference is with greater emphasis of being disturbed, past memory or Anxiety can do this. Two common places used to centre your Yi are your nose tip and the Lower Dantien-Xia. With focused Yi onto the tip of your nose, first you open your eyes to let spirit out, and draw your attention of eyes and nose; your eyes focus on the tip of the nose, activating the optic nerves and your Tai Yin point between your eyebrows. This connects energy directly back into your brain thinking mechanisms. This readjustment creates a valve of release for built up thought intrusions, whilst still paying attention to your breathing.
Gradually, the generation of new intrusive thoughts will cease.
Alternatively, concentrate your Yi on the Lower Dantien 'Xia', feeling and sensing the movement of Qi. Eventually, your thoughts will return to Serene calm.
These are done in a fairly quick moment, as you adjust and close your eyes again, seeping back into mind relaxation.

Restrain the Xin and Stop Method: Once you have bound your mind to one place, you must calm it down; otherwise, it will continue to interfere, you must prevent thoughts from being generated by the Xin. Understand why the (Xin) is still restless, this may simply be because of, or due to hunger or previous exercises - Qigong has not settled enough, and address these reasons. Just as with before, to keep your mind tied and to reflect on become calm, you must empathise with understanding awareness, to solve these meditation problems. That is when your calm serenity of 'body and mind thinking' can gradually settle.

To Comprehend these Real Stop Thought Methods: This final step in stopping thought involves analysing the continual generation of Xin and Nian (emotive intrusive thoughts).

Once you understand why the mind behaves restlessly, you can determine how to calm it. Only after calming your mind, can you guide Xin to understand and grasp the nature of reality. Meditation is a process, your mind, will get used too. Eventually, new disturbances of your Xin will cease. Educating the mind to understand that staying with the program brings your mind to a safe place, corresponds to your process. At this point, you no longer need to bind the mind. Achieving real regulation means keeping Xin and Nian from running wild, allowing Yi to direct them effortlessly.

Three Looks to Calm the Mind: There are three approaches to observing or investigating your thoughts, known as the Three Looks. When your mind is calm and peaceful, focus on your thoughts and learn to analyse them.

The Empty Look: (Kong Guan) When using the Empty Look, investigate, see the universe; how it originates, grows, changes, and eventually ceases. Through observation, understand the causes and effects of phenomena. Ultimately, everything is transient. According to the teachings I received at 'Sydneys Kadampa Buddhists Temple', of where I trained in beginning meditation, the desires stemming from the emotional mind are impermanent, called delusions and ultimately achieve nothing. Recognising this helps; stops the generation of new Xin and Nian.

The False Look (Jia Guan) represents false or imaginary. In this method, during a challenging situation like being stuck in traffic, instead of becoming frustrated or angry; try a reflection on how the jam formed in the past, then predict its resolution in the future. By focusing on these unreal aspects (not as yet seen), you can ease unsettling emotions and control Xin in the present. Past traumas can be debilitating like that, so remember they have passed and reason; why you now can move on-towards. Knowing thoughts can also come from outside energy, whose perspective has an agenda, not of your own. Be aware that not all energy or thoughts originate through the self, but can attach as does sound or smell.

The Centred Look (Zhong Guan): Using the first two 'Looks' we understand emotional disturbances, perceive emotional feelings, desires, as temporary. With this realisation, focus now on the present moment. Use your Yi to guide Xin into truths about our feelings, ensuring they no longer trouble mindful intent Yi.

Behold and Think Method (Guan Xiang Fa) "Guan" means "to admire" or "to view," and "Xiang" means "to imagine" or "to think." In this technique, concentrate on a loved personal objective or vision of say 'like a waterfall at moonlight'; to steady your Xin and regulate your mind. Focusing on this technique can give you images that empowers you to conquer the emotional mind. In past trainings, things such as, relax to the vision of a candle burning, with focus, then direct your vision inwards with eyes closed, once viewed of this candle burning. Allows thought to serenade into your mind peaceably.

The One Point Spiritual Enlightenment Method (Yi Dian Ling Ming Fa) "Yi Dian" refers to a single point, and "Ling" denotes the supernatural part of Shen (spirit), while "Ming" means "enlightenment." Here, focus on the highest level of Shen (spirit), directing it to a point in your Upper Wellness centre Shang (third eye). This effort stabilises Xin, fostering peace and calmness.

The Large Hand Stamp Method (Da Shou Yin) "Da Shou Yin" originates with Indian Buddhists and is widely used in Tibetan Qigong. By pressing fingers together in specific ways 'Mundra's, Mantras or Mudra', you can concentrate your mind on the point of contact. Establish a temporal shift inline with your training platform, perspective or destination. This method raises Shen and stops distracting thoughts. Shouting or generating sounds can also awaken Shen during meditation.I have seen and heard Religious practitioners often regulate their minds by lifting Shen. Through chanted prayer or even people in need to realise, release will just shout! As I am not religion tied, but do understand most things in this world needed some powerful embellishment of practice to survive into longevity? With Dragon Fire Qigong the "Ohm Ahh Hun" (Mind-Brain; soul-breath-voiced, Heart-harmony) connect our universal self.
    A meditation within this book 'Meditations and Meditative Stretching' as one of these.

My development in some Meditations taught to me at the Kadampa Tibetan Buddhist Temple Sydney; and from one of the Nine recommended meditation forms practiced as a beginning to Buddhist style mind harmony. I have of course developed this into my style of Dragon Fire Qigong meditations. As I do not follow the process of religions delivery. Along with this Meditation; is 'Simply Breathe' and return to 'Spirit Light'.

Above-Derived-is 'Understanding the Mental Body'; from a letter to the world found on the internet, Fr; Dr Yang Jing-Ming: I have changed its words and expression, but not the knowledge base; done to further suit my style of western meditative thinking, that I utilise within Dragon Fire. I must note he is one of the Masters I had chosen, as a learning from others being Masterful and accomplished in this world.

Dragon Fire Qigong

Meditations Harmony and Balanced Stretching

Mindfulness

Meditation

Below is the meditation posture and Mudra "Dragon Settles." The thumb, index and middle finger tips touch to unify the calming of Spirit- Pericardium; Lungs and Large Intestine meridians, this allows for harmony and balance of our 'Soul Breath' in meditation. Rest hands and fingers in 'Calm Serene 'and allow the words of Mindfulness meditations to be absorbed.

SECTION VIII:

MINDFULNESS and MEDITATIONS

Chapter 1:

Mindfulness

Meditation

From the teachings of 'Thich Nhat Hanh,' a disciple in these modern days, within the movement of Mindfulness Meditation! Rooted in the essence of Buddha's teachings (Buddhism), emerges 'Calm, Ease, Smile, Breathe', the artful joy of Mindful meditation and joyous being-fulfilment.
    This is a form of Mindfulness Meditation upon which I have based my concept of 'A Mindfulness Meditation approach', to lead onto the following stages of Nei gong.

Mindfulness for joyful living; can be described in this way: 'Within us!' There are many provisions of which to provide happiness and joyful being, both in and around us. Thus, if one is not Mindful of these abilities within or around us, the delivery into happiness and joy is greatly diminished, and left only to the immediate response to stimuli, that encroach on and/or pass through our living memories formed.

We as people, can be so caught up in the everyday living, that we forget to see, to feel, to breathe, to share with that which is all around, in the sense of life and Nature. Gestures of our worth in human connections; from the simple things, like a fellow greeting or a smile in passing. The sense of Mindfulness is to connect us to the smell of the flowers or trees, to feel the sunshine and wonder at the cloud shapes forming above, such as seen in this beautiful blue sky. Hearing the sound of a bird song, then look to see and find its presence, being of natural joy forming in the now, yet also in the living memories? Now for future calling.

So with most things in this life, we need to train, learn, and accumulate new things into our perceptions. Mindfulness training is one of these.

From this Meditation form, one will be able to acquire a better sense of (Calming the Body, Breath, and Mind). Intrinsically, one also needs this to accomplish a higher level of Qigong fulfilment in practice.

With this Mindfulness Meditation, we learn a new habit. We learn a way of truly relaxing and coming back to our present moment! To reflect on and with the ease of 'Calm, Ease, Smile, Breathe,' become as one with the joy of now.

Meditation begins in an easy sitting posture of relaxation.
To focus on the now and the breathe through the gentle sense of

connecting your mind and breath, rehearse the process of these simple words in stages: Mind connects to relaxation and the calming of our breathing.

Stage one: In/Out. As you breathe in, think 'In,' as you breathe out, think 'Out.' Continue this in/out breathing calmly and feel at ease with your breath and mind in this position.

Stage Two: Deep/Slow. As you breathe in, breathe more deeply, and when you breathe out, do it more slowly, so as to feel this breath sensation connecting to your intrinsic mindful sense.

Stage Three: Calm/Ease. As you breathe in now, sense the calm that your 'Breath, Body, and Mind' are feeling. As you breathe out now, feel the breathing has eased all tension within you.

Stage Four: Smile/Release. As you breathe in, smile deeply within, knowing this joyous feeling is you. When breathing out, release all sense of tension or angst as your body fills with joyous being.

Stage Five: Present Moment/Wonderful Moment. We end with 'Present moment' as we breathe in; how present it is to sense this joyful ease of feeling within. As we breathe out, how wonderful it is to feel such joyful ease in which we are right now. In this moment, such as it is, Mindfulness now.

To practice this sense of 'Calm, Ease, Smile, Breathe' is an integral part of what our bodies and minds require to fully appreciate the benefits and reflections that Dragon Fire Qigong can help one to acquire. Also, within the spectrum of 'Dragon Fire Qigong' are the more tranquil Nei Gong forms, and as we now have the place of sensing, relaxed, and within our body form in sitting. These meditations will flourish profoundly! 'Enjoy'.

Chapter 2:

Dragon Fire Qigong meditations

The purpose of meditation is to help let our minds sense the calm and peaceful. If our mind is peaceful, we can begin as if we are free from worries and mental distress or discomforts. So when we've experienced good periods of mental rest. We also developed the inner sense, that we can and should look to perform more ways to function this way.
    Within our ability to rest the mind-field of our very existence, in this our everyday life. Even the smallest amount of rest time gives the mind a break.
    Therefore, if we train in meditation, our mind will gradually perceive what mental peace really is. This will create a more purer sense of our knowing truth within our mental needs.

Simply Breathe Meditation
Sense the Breath

Using this basic breathing meditation, brings us to the first stage, of helping to disengage the mind from the busyness of everyday life. Develops; creates a special feeling of our soul breathe within lifes inner peace.

When our mind is in a peaceful state, we naturally feel happier, more contented and able to relax- this has a positive influence on everything we think, say or do.

As with any meditation though? The key to success is to be clear about what your objective is. Peaceful mind, less thought field dilemmas? Try to gain a better sense of your joyous heart! Simple breath is just that, keep your attention focused on it.

There will be a great temptation to follow your thoughts but try to resist this and remain focused single-pointedly on the breaths sensation. If you discover that your mind has wandered and is following your thoughts, immediately return it to the breath.
    Focus attention; to feel the coolness of breath as you inhale on the nostrils, then the warm release of breath.
    Repeat this as many times as necessary until your mind settles on the sensation of the breath and practice patiently in this way, gradually your distracting thoughts will subside and you will experience a sense of inner peace and relaxation.

Your mind will feel refreshed; lucid and spacious, stay with this state of mental calm for the remainder of the meditation.

Meditations Harmony and Balanced Stretching

The benefits of meditation: by practicing patiently and over a good amount of time. The discovery in your ability to sense inner peace and contentment, just by controlling the energy of your mind- without dependance on external conditions. Lets your mental mind realise true subsidence from turbulence in our mind scape.

Knowing we can become still, with a deep sensed calm serenity happening and calm spacious feeling within the mind, just by doing breathing meditations. Shows the Spirit self within our Soul breath; that not all environments we are placed in, deserve total control over ourselves.

Difficult situations, with digress emotive attachments of entanglement, can subside and a clear perspective of living joyously within can reappear.

Below is the Meditation Posture- Mudra for "Simple Breathe and Ohm Aah Hun" representing our sense of "Calm Serene'- In Body, Mind and Breath sensed.

Connect our universal self
Ohm Aah Hun Meditation

This special breathing meditation is designed to bring the body self, within a connection to our new simple breathe 'calm serene'. The life energy focus of moving the Heart/mind Xin, with the breath and inner silent Voice union of our Heart/mind/body.

Like an inner seed of self knowing, we focus our inner strength in supporting our life energy, with wind (prana) movement at and from our heart centre.

Thereby; using the construct of forging through the bodies sense to gain this deeper control over extraneous thought intrusions. This as the basis of many Buddhist- Yogic or Eastern meditation practice. Using the 'OM AHH HUN' as the essence of energy focused in the mantra.

The nature of- as such is; of enlightenment, speech and mind.

In this meditation you adjust the rhythm of your breathing so that you breathe in, hold your breath within **Xin**- Heart/mind, then breathe out.

You breathe in once more, and deliver the mind felt breath up to ascend into your brain- cerebellum, inwardly citing OM, move with this breath to your nostrils and as you breath out inwardly citing AHH until the sense of breath in your throat, releasing breath descends and has reached your heart/mind Xin once more inwardly citing HUN.

OM is the universal energy sense or our Celestial presence felt Shen.
AHH is the sound of the Soul breath- Po voiced in harmony connects to heart.
HUN is the name of our Ethereal Spirit connects- resides in our earthly body, as in Qigong- housed in the liver to feed the Heart blood Spirit- Qi Xue. Our Heart is the Spirit Vitality that allows our vibrance being, it is also represented as the Heavenly field- Dantian of Spirit, the centre of our earthly body energy fields, but connects to Spirit Light immortal.

OM AHH HUM in Yoga.

Meditations Harmony and Balanced Stretching

Return to Spirit Light Meditation
Absorbed into the light

Body of Light: as our breath and our body has merged into meditations; we then bring the sense of ourselves into Spirit. In Spirit Light eternal we represent the forging through our earthly self- Hun ethereal; our last tie to this earthly embodiment.

As within my 'Dragon Fire' I see Spirit light, as the Spirit Light immortal, that which when has passed through enlightenment. Knows to return to spirit is the guided pathway.

This practice meditation is to show a way in which we return to Spirit light, in our consciousness and want of delivery; for 'true loving joyous worth' from within becomes us.

This connection is a base from which many religious formulations have depended on through millennia? Vast amounts of time have been utilised in this world for the design of and of which in itself is infinitesimal time.

So our development is to realise a pathway of copying, a need to register more connection to within this eternal sense of hope, love, caring heart or establishing connections to our loved ones, within a world of which is not always caring.

We strengthen within ourselves and within our minds, through meditations that suit an individuals purpose. Therefore, this final merge of our 'spirit self soul breath' is the penetrating form of re-union, from light within and cleansed thought, mind into spirit joy, happiness and the ultimate statement of fulfilment. Recognising your true worth!

With this meditation we lay a foundation for our meditating on the mind by helping to temporarily overcome physical appearances. To relax our energy channels and balance inner energy (winds) upon which the mind is connecting.

To start we engage the body in its normal form, seeing ourselves as if from outside - yet from within us at once. How we look, how we feel, our state of life measure in person. We know we are made up of skin and bone, blood and tissues, with many working parts. So what if we were to then imagine that the contents of our physical being, is being felt by the sky, the shining sun or the celestial presence.

If we were to look up into a blue sky directly at the Sun, we become unable to see anything but bright light. This is the sense now; of what we hope to achieve within this meditation.

An ability of releasing your embodied self to the imagined merging into the light. And by doing so imagine your physical body becomes light- bright white transparent, with a shell presenting as Spirit self and all the dilemmas of your physical body, with ailments, mental stress; of emotive thoughts, all these can dissipate, be absorbed into the light.

Released from the unsettling element of thinking. We begin to reabsorb through the light, just as we would through our spirit light eternal, become cleansed free of burdens of lifes struggles. To once again feel the sensed knowing, that you are more than just struggles, heart aches or a performance that suits other energy.

This is a meditation of which if developed, to instil your sense of having an energy platform; a Spirit Self, you could look to find hidden harmony and life balance. Returning once again to the now as an invigorated reunited self worth.

Beginning your daily journeys and with knowing now that you have an ability within, to seek change and restructure within a simple platform, a simple easy life style pathway leading to joyous wellness from deep within.

Meditations Harmony and Balanced Stretching

Dragon Fire Qigong

SECTION IX:

DRAGON FIRE QIGONG

MANAGING ENERGY

THROUGH THE "WATER MIND" OF INTENT

Dragon Fire Qigong

Chapter 1:

Managing Energy through the "Water Mind" of Intent

The postnatal aspect of Spirit/Self that governs our daily lives and is known as the "human mind," with its two distinctly different facets. One as the "Mind of Emotion" or "Fire Mind," which resides in the heart (Xin). The other as the "Mind of Intent," or "Water Mind," which resides in the head (Yi) and common-sense. Likened to Fire, this mind of emotion is volatile, hot, and unpredictable, as our thoughts can quickly run out of control. Especially with connection to things like; love, sex, or partnerships? Along with the many constraints, of family and working environments.

As we may know? These connections tend to run quickly out of control and can be easily inflamed by the presence of external stimuli, or state of current affairs that have an impact on our general day to day life harmony.

Therefore, these thoughts and actions formed within lifes unexpected series of events. Couple then within the normality of generating our sense of sporting or energetic pastimes. Such as energetic-vibrational risings; due to strenuous exercise or- summer heat, will rise and fuse to your brain or chest, creating turmoil of energy tied to thought in- actioned.

By contrast, the mind of Intent is like Water: clear, cool, calm, capable of reflecting "the cosmos" and the great absorber, without disturbing its own nature. While the Fire mind is linked directly to the five senses and responds emotionally to the constant play of sensory perceptions, the Water mind, when still and silent, enjoys direct access to the infinite wisdom and awareness of the primordial Spirit and Yuan Qi. In the deeper recesses of our makeup and intuitiveness, is the capacity to unfold calming, caring or sensible arrays of uniformity and promise.

Intent in this faculty, by which the Water mind may take control of the human system- override, and lessen the effects of harmful and explosive Fiery intentions. One of the primary goals of Qigong then is to learn how to harness the Fiery passions, with wisdom's calming control, to use Intent to manage energy, rather than allowing energy to be wasted by emotions beyond sensibility. By transforming essence into energy, refining energy, and raising it up through the spinal channels into the head, then transforming energy into Spirit connect.

We accomplish an awareness and nurturing, to enhance the power of Intent to control emotions. Once this has been achieved, the second phase of internal alchemy can be practiced, whereby spirit commands energy, and energy commands essence. Meaning that the mind gains control over the body through the medium of energy, realising primordial power of "mind over matter" is a construct of thought, of which needs extra awareness in developing; mind safety first is principled.

The ultimate stage of self-cultivation and internal alchemy is to fathom the mysteries and awareness of the awakened spirit. At the core of all Qigong practice- dynamic or tranquil, Martial, Healing, or Spiritual -lies the deep pondering pool of eternal wisdom of the "Water Mind element." So, as was stated from a time gone past, in the immortal words of wisdom, *"When Spirit takes command, the body naturally follows it, and this arrangement benefits all Three Treasures. When the body leads the way, the Spirit trails along, and this damages all Three treasures."* Metaphorically, the "Three Treasures" are like the three planes of our being in one: a physical body, an emotional connect, and a mental connect. With this in mind, delve into the structure of:

The Four Stages of Knowing:

One must be awakened; to an Awareness Being, in Spirituality, and Enlightenment follows.

Chapter 2

The Forming of Energy Within: Dragon Fire Qigong

When one has practiced enough routines and techniques within this form of Qigong, the body starts to sense a new type of feeling—that which is the forming of transformational intrinsic Qi energy. This energy can be felt inside your body, and through accumulations of Mind-Body-Breath, it becomes noticeable in the ability to forge elemental energy throughout the body. Additionally, as the mind becomes healthier, the internal sense of wellness and joyous being forms, accomplishing healing, restoration, and harmonious internal connection.

Having fully enjoyed my accumulation of awareness and body transformation from deep illness and injury to a point of knowing that this art of Dragon Fire Qigong has resurrected the worth in my life, I have always sensed a need to be. And now, knowing that this art of Qigong offers an eternal journey of discovery for both Spirit and Self in joyous being, and in the ability to help others reconnect with their own hopes and preferences for exercise, mindfulness, and vitality, producing elemental worth that captures the purest joy of living—knowing yourself from within.

I sincerely hope that those whom have the opportunity to read this book "Meditations- Harmony and Balanced Stretching" and in the realisation of how I developed and discovered my own sense of fulfilment find it beneficial. I look forward to future partnerships focused on vitality, wellness, and joyous being through my art of 'Dragon Fire Qigong.'

Yours sincerely,

Marc Harry Creator, Instructor, Teacher

CONCLUSION

A. Re-emphasise the key points

Foundations of Qigong	4
Correct Postures- Holding to Form	6
Directing the Qi	15
Meditation Techniques	18
Warming the Balance	27
How to Find the Qi	48
Context of Five Elements- Dragon Fire Qigong	57
Simple in Practice	64
Yin Yang	68
Seated Seed Conception Form 8 Tri Gram + Centre	81
Bāguà to Feng Shui	87
Longevity Forms	94
Ba Duan Jin Seated Essence	126
The Three Locks for Meditation	151
Understanding the Mental Body	157
Dragon Fire Qigong Meditations-	169
Managing Energy through the "Water Mind" of Intent	177

B. Explain what you hope the reader takes away from the book

My hope is that you are someone whom can see the benefit of learning from someones inspiration, or story and then implement the strategies, platforms and principle practices of 'Dragon Fire ' Qigong. This is a construct of my own survival in a sense of adapting to environmental forces, generally beyond an individuals sense of achieved. To find that implementing your own connections of "Healing Recovery or Wellness" from another's learnings. In this case the book that you are reading, one of a series: this being; (Dragon Fire Qigong: Meditations Harmony and Balanced Stretching).

I also hope that your direction into a sense of meditation, calming your inner self and the possibility of you, becoming harmonised into your better Spirit/Self, unites with the purpose of all who want to find inner peace, harmony balanced and Wellness in your life.

C. Any final closing thoughts

These principles of development of my Spirit Self and my personifications of deliverance from hurt, trauma and illness has been made possible. Firstly because I'd recognised within my own sense of hope for joyous wellness and balanced harmony, that I was the one that needed to make the choice. Change and awareness of what it is sensed deep inside of me. Secondly; I'd felt in spite of my environment causing harm. That I should also pursue my betterment, with an understanding that others suffer from an environment of energy, that which can bring harmful- hurting affects into their connection of life experience too.
    So, within this my dilemma "resilience can be inspiration to yourself." Therefore find your pathway to happiness of living worth, inspire your friendships with living Earth and accommodate your own sensing of Joyous Wellness from deep within.

Meditations Harmony and Balanced Stretching

Dragon Fire Qigong

Book:
Bibliography:
In an order of appreciation! Understand that it would not have been possible for me to undergo this wellness performing change in my life, without the previous formulations and theory that has accumulated through our societies over time. Special mention must be made. Although I have created my own form of Healing style of Qigong? Through the absorption of others words and concepts. Therefore; special mention is toward those people whom books or DVDs, became a knowledge base, and even though I needed to adapt, change, or perform things differently.

I had to firstly find, that such a thing as "Qigong" and "Nei gong" and then as this following sequence reveals. Nei Dan Gong existed. So! As I have had very little education; due to my life circumstance, therefore; and as a twenty-year-old I created the ability; through the study of some books to try and heal and revitalise my body and mind, after a deathly incident had become a destruction upon me. I used some books I purchased.

Those books were from the author Robert W Smith: a series of three books: on Chinese Internal boxing. (Techniques of Hsing-I & Pa-Kua). And Cheng Man Ch'ing: 37 posture Tai Chi Ch'uan. [Sadly, I was run over by a drunk driver and destroyed again two years later].

But then; twenty eight years later: I took the memory of those books and started to create my own form of Three Links: Chi Boxing; to help survive a dilapidating, depressive and physically injurious body, all from the advent of those many years before! And more hardships that followed- had befallen me.

This new search then began from the point of-'now knowing'-that I had discovered Qigong from a book I'd purchased- The Healing Promise of Qi whilst staying at my sister's home recovering; being left homeless and unwell after a 'cyclone- Yasi' wreaked havoc on my life. Then from within many libraries I studied, whilst suffering off and on homelessness and through a constant struggle; I was able to attach a learning wellness program, through books and DVDs, accessible from these public libraries. As the internet had grown into the many opportunities, allowing so much that an individual could discover and utilise what was existing out there in the greater world.

In this my continuing pursuit to search, I discovered a complete visual platform, and some of these came from a person I later met in Sydney.
Simon Blow: his series of Books/DVDs are what gave assistance and insight to then enable myself to become "Dragon Fire Qigong."

These became a base of my knowledge of, and understanding, and

Meditations Harmony and Balanced Stretching

parts of my adaptations into "Dragon Fire" came from these influences.

There are others and even though as stated: I have created my own form of "Chi Boxing; Qigong." I need to state that before I was run over all those years ago, I had attended many training venues and trained with multiple Masters styles in martial Arts. I was run over the day after teaching my first student.

Now that I was putting my ideas of training recovery and wellness into a practice! These forms had to be made into a book form to keep my knowledge gained and to continue growing my abilities.

Firstly! My Chi Boxing forms; (This is my "Soul Defence" becomes).

My Qigong style at first had to be created without the opportunities that others had; to enlist the teaching from others as their guide and instructor. But, I did have opportunities to watch them on DVDs. Therefore; I have seen enough to know what movements look like, and the words explain the presence of becoming, through decades I might add of studying, becomes that meaning in oneself.

Thus I created my Qigong to suit my needs; of healing from within, following guidelines that I've seen, and constructed my own formations of, to become Spirit/Self within healing, restoration, vitality, and joyous being.

As was mentioned? I have had very little educational opportunity, therefore I have had to learn words and ways from other peoples' books. But I have created in my own sense; the formulations into book form. I feel that I can reveal my intrinsic art of becoming Spirit/Self reformed, by an avenue that has no ties to a negative or bad influence. But can show that a light of worth, has come from the many whom, I have selected to learn words and ways from.

Some of the many Books, DVDs that I have used to capture knowledge and learning will be listed below. All of them I had found to be enlightening and fulfilling, in their own right! But, I have had this deep internal need to survive in my own self-worth, and ability. And so; therefore, this is why I've created my own style to resurrect my living worth, and through this opportunity of having a home to rest up in for a time? I must state this is not the first of my constructs into book form, but will be the first I try to present to this world.

The books most used; in order to keep my style attached, to a true pathway already made, are:
Absorbing the Essence: Simon Blow - Genuine Wisdom Centre.
The Art of Life: Simon Blow - Genuine Wisdom Centre.
Restoring Natural Harmony: Simon Blow - Genuine Wisdom Centre.
(I attended a Qigong class of Simon's, when I was first homeless in Sydney, then when returning to Sydney, became a full-time trainee,

now a qualified Teacher Trainer level 4 from some of his Qigong).
So more; Six Unity Qigong Simon Blow Genuine Wisdom Centre.
Da Wu health: book-DVD, Qigong Da Wu exercise; Chinese Health Qigong Association.
Chi-kung: Harnessing the Power of the Universe; Daniel P. Reid 1948.
Healing self-massage: Kristine Kaoweri Weber.
Qigong Illustrated: Christina J. Barea.
Qigong Massage: Master Yang. Jwing - Ming. (parts from books and DVDs over time from him; White Crane Hard and Soft Qigong purchased)
The Healing Promise of Qi: Roger Janke, O.M.D.
(A book I purchased)
DVD Infinite Chi Kung for Health: Jason Chan.
DVDs: Ba Gua Zhang Vol one & two by Par Jean - Jacques Galinier. (I purchased)
DVD: Yi Jin Jing; Qi Productions. Master Tang Lai Wei. (Purchased)
A series of books also from Master Mantak Chia of which I invest understanding and awareness from these.
Energy Balance through the Tao Mantak Chia; Advanced Chi Nei Tsang Mantak Chia; Iron Shirt Chi Kung 1 Mantak Chia. Plus more...
The Web That Has No Weaver by Ted J. Kaptchuk, O.M.D. Gifted by a friend.
The Foundations of Chinese Medicine Third edition Giovanni Maciocia- gifted by a good friend-the same 'Anita'.

These being that which I utilised when using help through the many library systems or purchases I had made in recent years, and after finding Qigong.

Above are the books and DVD's I have used to formulate the wordings and paraphrase the in-depth knowledge of Qi; Qigong and Nei gong into books of my own style "Dragon Fire Qigong." There are so many more, one of the benefits in my younger years was to learn from the copious books and styled techniques on offer from this world. Many masters did I study and train with back in those days also (Martial Art- Daoist Philosophy).

As I have only had the opportunity for a short time, to no-longer be broken and homeless, struggling in hardship or poverty. I have to state that when I was reading and researching over the years, through the many libraries that were on offer around me. I had no idea at that time, that I would accomplish creating such a fine example, of restructuring a life in essence, from such hardship and inability to find peace.

So many other books and movies, or documents, or DVDs and the like, have become "that which I am" engrained into the perceived reality that I fulfil as "Dragon Fire." I truly hope that this

Meditations Harmony and Balanced Stretching

explanation is sufficient enough, to allow the deep respect that I have for these people, whom have allowed in essence, an opportunity for someone such as I, to be able to produce a living worth in essence! To become again; a need to inspire through self-learning, a connection to the beauty and living hope, and worth that must exist somewhere in this universe-that surrounds my living presence, and heartfelt need to find Spirit/Self in living worth.

A further note! If at all someone gets the opportunity to read these other books:

[Three Links: Chi Boxing. Dragon Fire; Qigong; Nei gong. Dragon Fire Qigong; Meditations Harmony Forged Five Elements and Eight Tri Grams Meditative Stretching].

I ask! That they take into account my life felt circumstance; and understand that I have not really had the professional opportunity in education, to flourish as a person whom has been taught the correct procedures, of formulating a knowledge base book, and so, from the principle of extracting from other peoples works-sources? So my order of apology is placed:

I have had to learn by studying from the words, ways and essence of others, deriving the truth in my awareness by application, and in so doing actually grew the knowledge of these, also deep within my persona and skilful capabilities. I therefore became "Dragon Fire" itself by becoming skilful in what this world revealed, and by my actions to create knowing worth in my ability. My skills had to be adapted by my own cognisance, from a practice delivery I put together in libraries all over this country I lived.

I taught myself how to read and edit and produce a sense of skill required to perform at a higher level, and my training in spelling, computer check? And editing; all through assistance supplied in Libraries. This particular book is because I was fortunate enough to receive generous support from a particular person, she- Ugné, whom helped me become more knowledgeable and capable with modern technology (computers; phones, apps and the internet).

With this in mind, their knowledge gifted to me, and my rehearsing them into my persona, was a most proficient way of learning, and also the best sense of instruction, that could be offered to another's opportunity to become, as I have, into "Dragon Fire."

So once again. Thank you; and with sincerity, from Marc Harry. Creator; instructor, teacher of - Three Links: Chi Boxing; and my- Dragon Fire Qigong/Nei gong. 'If you are reading this book; please enjoy'.

Dragon Fire Qigong

Meditations Harmony and Balanced Stretching

Dragon Fire Qigong

Meditations Harmony and Balanced Stretching

www.ingramcontent.com/pod-product-compliance
Lightning Source LLC
Chambersburg PA
CBHW061727070526
44583CB00024B/3038